Settling the Score

TALKIN' CHICAGO SPORTS

Mike North

TRIUMPH
BOOKS

Library of Congress Cataloging-in-Publication Data

North, Mike, 1952–
    Settling the score : talkin' Chicago sports / Mike North.
    p. cm.
    ISBN 978-1-60078-193-3
  1. Sports—Illinois—Chicago—History. I. Title.
    GV584.5.C4N67 2009
    796.09773'11—dc22

2009005080

This book is available in quantity at special discounts for your group or organization. For further information, contact:

Triumph Books
542 South Dearborn Street
Suite 750
Chicago, Illinois 60605
(312) 939-3330
Fax (312) 663-3557
www.triumphbooks.com

Printed in U.S.A.
ISBN: 978-1-60078-193-3
Design by Sue Knopf
Photos courtesy of AP Images unless otherwise indicated
Author photos courtesy of Alex Goykhman

Contents

About the Author

RAISED IN CHICAGO'S ROGERS PARK NEIGHBORHOOD, Mike North's first real job was as a hot dog vendor at Wrigley Field and Comiskey Park in 1969. After a stint in the military and several jobs with the city of Chicago, North capitalized on his talent for serving hot food and spicy sports talk and opened his hot dog stand, Be-Be's, in 1985.

Among North's frequent customers was the staff of Diamond Broadcasting, owners of WXRT-FM and WSBC-AM. After suggesting the idea of a sports show to the Diamond management team, North launched the "NFL Handicap Show" on WSBC in 1990. In 1992, the first Chicago-based sports radio station, The Score Sports Radio WSCR-AM 820, was born. North was offered a job to host a radio show with former Chicago Bears player, Dan Jiggetts, and soon they became "The Monsters of the Midday," delivering a unique brand of opinionated, street-smart sports talk to Chicago sports fans.

In September 1999, The Score changed signals and line-ups. The frequency became 1160 AM, and North began hosting his own show, "The Mike North Show," from 12:00 to 4:00 PM Monday through Friday. "My show is like sports with all the trimmings," said North of his show, "it's everything you want—exactly how you want it."

In August 2000, The Score once again changed frequencies, this time to 670 AM—its current station. Two years later, North teamed up with another Chicago Bears alumnus, Doug Buffone, and they soon became known as "The Wise Guys."

In September 2004, North moved from the midday to the morning. He worked this time slot with Fred Huebner until June 2008 when he chose not to accept the deal offered to him by The Score's management.

Mike North has gone one-on-one with many well-known sports figures including Pete Rose, Dick Butkus, Walter Payton, and Wilt Chamberlain, while hosting his TV shows. North has won two Emmy Awards, one for his *North Side* segments on FOX-TV, and one for *Primetime TV Show*. North has won four Achievement in Radio Awards. He was named Radio Broadcaster of the Year in 1996. North and Dan Jiggetts received the awards for Best Midday Show in Chicago and Best Sports Show in 1997, and North won Best Talent on a News, Talk, Personality, or Sports Station in 2002.

Mike North's other accomplishments include receiving the Entertainer of the Year Award from the Special Children's Charities, the Irv Kupcinet Award by the Ed Kelly Giant Awards, and the Richard J. Daley Award by the Red Cloud Athletic Fund. His persistence in bringing 16" softball, a game he loves to play, to the Chicago high school system as a varsity sport earned him the 1999 Man of the Year Award from the Softball Hall of Fame. He was selected by the Board of Directors of the National Ethnic Coalition of Organizations to be the recipient of the prestigious 2004 Ellis Island Medal of Honor. In 2005, North won a Telly Award for a commercial. He won the Silver Circle Award from the National Conference for Community and Justice of Chicago and Greater Illinois. He was honored as a 2006 inductee into the Chicagoland Sports Hall of Fame—the first radio broadcaster ever to be inducted. He also received the 2006 Media Excellence Award from the National Italian American Sports Hall of Fame. North is the assistant basketball coach at Notre Dame High School. He sat in for Don Imus on WFAN in New York. Steve Stone, noted broadcaster, commented recently that Mike North is the best one-on-one interviewer he has ever heard. North has conducted over 13,000 interviews. Jesse Jackson and Mike North worked together to persuade the Chicago Cubs to erect a statue honoring Mr. Cub, Ernie Banks. It was dedicated on Opening Day 2008. He was featured on HBO's *Bob Costas Now* as one of the premier sports radio hosts in the country.

North left The Score in 2008. He was the first broadcaster to do a live web show from a private business website, wildfirerestaurant. com. He writes a column with Dan Jiggetts for the *Chicago Sun-Times*. Currently, North is executive producer and co-host of *The Monsters in the Morning* on Comcast SportsNet airing Monday through Friday from 6:00 to 9:00 AM, and he can be heard live on the web at Chicagosportswebio.com

North is a partner and executive vice president of Chicagosports-webio.com, an Internet sports-talk station.

Mike North and his wife, Be-Be, live in the northwest suburbs with their dog, Lucky, a black lab mix from the Anti-Cruelty Society.

Acknowledgments

I OWE STEVE SILVERMAN A HUGE DEBT OF GRATITUDE for his help in making this book come together. A hot dog salesman–turned broadcaster–turned author, left to his own resources, would be unlikely to produce anything worth reading, but with the help of an All-Pro collaborator he's at least in the game. And Steve is not just an All-Pro, he's an MVP.

Introduction

CHICAGO IS EASILY THE NO. 1 SPORTS CITY IN THE COUNTRY.

More than New York. More than Boston. More than Washington, Los Angeles, San Francisco—anywhere else.

Chicago is a city where all of the sports fans are located right in the city. Keeping the stadiums in Chicago has been the key to allowing this town to be the best for the fans.

They have some rabid fans in Boston and New York. I'm not going to deny that, but say those rabid fans want to go watch their beloved Patriots. Well, it's not like they are going to downtown Boston. They have to go to Foxborough, and that's an hour away and a lot more than that with traffic.

Same with New York. Okay, you want to go watch the Yankees, you go to Yankee Stadium in the Bronx. Fair enough. But if you want to go see the NEW YORK Giants or the NEW YORK Jets, you have to go to New Jersey.

There's nothing wrong with going to Foxborough to watch the Patriots or going over the bridge to Jersey to watch the Giants or Jets. But it's not the same as watching a game at Soldier Field right in the heart of Chicago.

The Cubs are in Wrigleyville, and the Sox are on the South Side. If you want to go see the Hawks or the Bulls, you go down Madison Street.

People went to see them play on Madison Street at the old Chicago Stadium when it was a very rough neighborhood and they still support them. You know why nobody talks about the Chicago Fire (Major League Soccer)? Because they don't play in Chicago. They play in Bridgeview. If I wanted to go see them play, I wouldn't have any idea where to go.

You have to play in the city limits. That's what Chicago has that New York and Boston don't. Maybe Philadelphia and St. Louis do as well, but there's no way that Chicago takes a back seat to those two—all due respect.

And this is not from a guy who simply thinks all things Chicago are great and all things from New York or Boston or Washington or San Diego are awful. I love New York. It's a great city. But they shouldn't call New York the city that never sleeps. I have been to New York many, many times and there are bars and restaurants that close up at 11:00 PM or 11:30 PM. Those are the facts.

You want a city that never sleeps? Take Boston. It's a great city. I like New York, and I can stay there for a few days at a time. I can go to Boston and spend a week there. But I can spend a lifetime here in Chicago, the greatest city in the world. Anything and everything you want, you can get in Chicago. The bars stay open until 2:00 AM, and it's beautiful.

It has everything. You want to tell me there's no ocean in Chicago; I'll give you Lake Michigan. It's better than any ocean. If I take somebody from California, blindfold them so they don't know where they are, and I bring them to Oak Street Beach, I can turn them around to face Lake Michigan and take off the blindfold. If I tell them to just look at the water on an 80-degree day and ask them where they are, they will say they are in California staring at the Pacific Ocean. A wise guy might say he is in Florida looking at the Atlantic Ocean. Lake Michigan is as big and beautiful as any ocean—at least when you are looking at it up close. Obviously the lake's not as big as the Pacific or Atlantic or any ocean, but when you're at the beach, it looks just like an ocean.

1

Bears

IS THERE ANYBODY WHO'S MORE OF A CHICAGO BEAR THAN MIKE DITKA?

Once you get past George Halas himself, there's nobody even close. Ditka is Da Coach, and before he was Da Coach, he was one of the best tight ends who ever played the game.

I loved Mike Ditka the player, and I loved Mike Ditka as a coach. And as far as being on the radio with him, I loved that, too.

But while having him on the air was good for Mike North and the Score, it was also good for Mike Ditka. I don't know that he ever acknowledged that. I have nothing but respect for Ditka, but that doesn't mean he didn't do a few things that really upset me, and I talked about them on the air.

After the 2006 season, it bothered me that the Bears were going into the NFC Championship Game against the Saints, the other team he had coached, and he never came out and said who he was backing. It was obvious that his ties to Chicago were a lot stronger than his relationship with New Orleans, so who was he kidding by not coming out and rooting for the Bears?

I was always on Ditka's side when he was coaching the Bears, even when things weren't going well for him in that last season. That was 1992, the first year the Score (WSCR-AM) was on the air. I backed him until the end, and I think he was appreciative of

Chicago Bears quarterback Jim McMahon, left, has a chat with head coach Mike Ditka, right, during first half action on January 5, 1986, in Chicago during the playoff game against the New York Giants. (AP Photo/John Swart)

that. The Bears were awful that season (5–11, tied for third in the NFC Central), and all the talk was about when Ditka would be fired, who would replace him, and how the team would react to a new coach. I had said all along that season that the Bears had better think long and hard about replacing Ditka. And if they did fire him, they couldn't come in with somebody who didn't at least come close to him in personality.

Well, leave it to Mike McCaskey to follow Mike Ditka with Dave Wannstedt. All the experts thought Wannstedt was this defensive genius for the Cowboys who would follow in Jimmy Johnson's footsteps and become this great coach. He was a disaster who couldn't carry Ditka's cigar case. Wannstedt didn't know what he was doing, and I guess that's what made him McCaskey's boy.

Before Ditka became George Halas' choice to coach the Bears—the last decision Halas made for the team before he died in 1983—he was a great player for the Bears. To me, he was one of the best tight ends who ever played in the NFL. He was a great blocker who would knock everybody down in front of him, and he had great hands. The guy is in the Hall of Fame, for crying out loud.

There have been other good tight ends, but when Ditka came along, he was the first one to be used as a pass receiver as well as a blocker on an almost equal basis. He was simply an unstoppable player once he caught the ball. Unlike a lot of players that you see nowadays, Ditka would not go down to the ground or run out of bounds. If you wanted to stop Ditka after he caught a pass, you had to tackle him. Usually it took two or three guys to stick him good if you wanted to tackle him.

That's one of the main reasons I liked Ditka so much. You can say that he demanded a lot of his players and that he was tough on them, but he never asked for more than he gave himself. And he gave it to the same franchise that he played for and made his name. Ditka didn't have to be such a hard-ass or such a tough guy, but that's what came naturally for him. He was being true to himself, and he was the right guy to coach the team when Halas brought him on board.

"Ditka didn't have to be such a hard-ass or such a tough guy, but that's what came naturally for him."

You have to remember where the Bears were before Ditka got there. They had been coached by Neill Armstrong for the previous four seasons—not exactly an inspirational guy. Armstrong may have been a nice guy, but I'm not sure how much the players listened to him. They were a losing team in their last two years under Armstrong, so it was obvious that they needed somebody with fire and passion. That's why Halas was willing to put past differences with Ditka aside and bring him back to the team.

For one, Ditka had the same philosophy as Halas on how to build a team. At the time, the passing game was really becoming popular. Ditka had seen for himself how damaging the passing game could be because he was an assistant coach for Tom Landry and the Cowboys and they had just been beaten by the 49ers in the NFC Championship Game on Dwight Clark's famous catch of Joe Montana's pass. But Ditka still thought that if you put together a team that could punish and pummel the opponent, you could win a game.

He pretty much said the same thing when Halas called him up, brought him to Chicago, and interviewed him about the possibility of becoming head coach of the Bears. Halas asked Ditka what his philosophy was about being a head coach in the NFL, and Ditka told him he didn't have a philosophy.

Instead, he told Halas that he was not going to throw the football all over the lot and that he didn't believe in doing that. Instead, he wanted to bring a nasty, tough team on the field and simply kick ass.

It was a simple answer, and it was the same kind of philosophy that Halas had when he was coaching the Bears and one that he believed in until the very end. That made the match between coach and owner a perfect one.

But Ditka knew that his attitude and personality were not a match for everyone in Halas Hall. Not all of the Bears' front office people agreed with Halas that the philosophy of pounding your opponent was going to win in the NFL. It didn't matter when Halas was alive and still the man that Ditka had to answer to, but once Halas died in 1983, Ditka had to deal with quite a bit of friction from the owner's box.

As he was molding his team in 1982 and 1983, Ditka was putting together a team of punishing, hard-hitting guys who were willing to run through a wall for him. By the time the 1984 season started, Bears fans knew that Ditka was on the right track with his team. There were a few games that season that let us know for sure that the Bears were on their way. There was a home game against Minnesota where the Bears absolutely murdered the Vikings. The score was only 16–7, but the defense basically kicked Minnesota quarterback Tommy Kramer all over the field. The Bears had 11 sacks that game, and you knew they were something special.

A week later, the Raiders came to Chicago. The Raiders were basically the bullies of the NFL. They had beaten the Redskins in the Super Bowl, and they were supposed to be tough. The Bears beat them 17–6 and also beat them up. Jim McMahon lacerated his kidney that game which ended up costing them, but it marked the changing of the guard in the NFL. The Bears were real, and everybody knew it.

The team proved it by going down to Washington and beating the Redskins in the playoffs, but they took it on the chin against the 49ers in the NFC Championship Game. It was a game that would stick with Ditka and the Bears for a long time. There were reasons for the loss, including McMahon's injury, but Ditka couldn't stomach the idea of losing to Bill Walsh.

After the game, Walsh handed out a couple of back-handed compliments to the Bears, saying they would be the team to beat once they got their offense squared away and McMahon came back. Ditka knew there was something pretty smug about Walsh even if he truly was a great coach. In the locker room after the game, Ditka told the team how much he believed in them and that they would take care of the 49ers next year.

That loss burned inside of Ditka throughout the whole off-season. He was particularly livid that they used offensive guard Guy McIntyre as a lead blocker from the fullback position. Ditka couldn't wait for the 1985 season to start, and he couldn't wait to take on the 49ers.

That happened early in 1985—the sixth game of the season. The Bears were rolling, having won the first five games of the year before the road trip to San Francisco. Not only was Ditka looking forward to this game, but so was everyone else. The offense was particularly motivated, having been insulted by Walsh following the NFC Championship Game the year before. The Bears overpowered the Niners on both sides of the ball, using the running of Walter Payton (132 yards) and the speed and aggressiveness of the defense to punish San Francisco. Joe Montana was sacked seven times in that game, and he never knew what hit him.

Ditka decided enough was not enough and wanted to pay Walsh back for the way he had used McIntyre the year before. He had his own secret weapon in William "the Refrigerator" Perry, and he lined him up in the backfield. It wasn't a play that the Bears had practiced, but Ditka wanted to send his own message to Walsh.

He called Perry over, told him he was going to run the ball and to protect the ball when he got hold of it. The Bears used Perry to run with the ball on two plays in a row, and he virtually took all the life out of the San Francisco defense. The 49ers wanted no part of the 325–330-pound Perry. You couldn't blame them, either!

So the Bears won the game, and Ditka sent his personal message to Walsh in the form of Perry running the ball. That victory had taken care of all past-due bills. Ditka knew it, and it was time to look forward to taking the team to new heights during the rest of the year. However, Buddy Ryan didn't appreciate the way Ditka had used his defensive tackle. Ryan didn't have much use for Ditka to begin with, but using Perry in the backfield was something the defensive coordinator viewed as stepping on his toes.

Ditka didn't care. He saw Perry as an offensive weapon, and he was going to continue to use him. If he didn't get along with his defensive coordinator, that didn't matter—all he really had to worry about was taking his team to the Super Bowl.

The rest of the season was a pretty smooth ride for the Bears, with dominating wins the rule most of the way. Who will ever be able to forget the 44–0 win over the Dallas Cowboys in Texas Stadium? I think that win may have shocked a lot of the older Bears and former players more than any game they played that year.

My old buddy Doug Buffone took more pleasure out of beating the Cowboys than any other team because Tom Landry and Roger Staubach had stuck it to them just about every time they played. So to go down to Dallas and punish the Cowboys like that was just a tremendous weapon. If they could beat the Cowboys like that on the road, how could anyone else stick with them?

That became the question the rest of the year. Could they go on to an undefeated season and win the Super Bowl? Could this be the best team of all time? Bears fans wanted it all, and so did Ditka. They were 12–0 when they went to Miami for that Monday night game in early December. The Dolphins had Dan Marino and a big-time passing game, but going into that game, you just had the feeling that the Bears were going to bury the Dolphins. They had done it to everybody else. They were getting better, and they just seemed like they were bigger, stronger, and tougher.

"Could they go on to an undefeated season and win the Super Bowl? Could this be the best team of all time?"

There would be no Jim McMahon, but they had been winning without him. Remember, that 44–0 win over Dallas came with Steve Fuller in the lineup. He was no McMahon, but he was capable. The Dolphins, however, were as ready for the Bears as any team that season. Instead of letting Marino sit in the pocket like he usually did, Don Shula had him

Defensive coach Buddy Ryan hugs linebacker Otis Wilson (55) as they watch the final seconds run off the clock in the Bears game against the New York Giants, on January 5, 1986, at Soldier Field in Chicago. (AP Photo)

roll out so he could buy time, stay away from the pass rush, and find open receivers.

The Dolphins got a few breaks in the game and took advantage of them, and that's why the final score was 38–24 Dolphins. Ditka couldn't have been more angry with Ryan because of the play of the defense, but there was no flaw there. It was just the circumstances of the game that got away from the Bears, and Miami took advantage.

There would be no hangover after losing that game. The Bears would close out the season with three more wins before rolling into the playoffs with a 15–1 record.

The first team in was the Giants, and I don't know what Phil Simms says now, but there was no way the Giants had a chance against that Bears team. It was a 21–0 shutout, and the Giants had no hope. It was the same thing the next week in the NFC Championship Game against the Rams. This time it was 24–0 as the Bears pummeled Eric Dickerson and treated him like he was some third-stringer. He couldn't do a thing, and he was by far the best running back in the league at the time—outside of Payton. The Rams' quarterback was Dieter Brock, a Canadian Football League refugee who had had a pretty good year. But he was not in the class of the Bears defense, and that was that.

The Bears finally had a shot at the Super Bowl, and Ditka was not about to blow it. This was the reason Halas had hired him to be head coach, and I know Ditka's only regret was that the Old Man was not there to enjoy it. The Patriots had gone on a great run to get to the Super Bowl as the AFC champs, but they had been handled 20–7 by the Bears in a game that wasn't as close as the score, and there was no way their next meeting would be any different.

Added to the motivation of the Bears winning the Super Bowl was the likelihood that Ryan was leaving to become a head coach elsewhere. That got the defense even more fired up than usual. When the two teams took the field at the Superdome in New Orleans on January 26, 1986, there was only one possible outcome.

There was one moment of hesitation. The Bears fumbled on the opening series of the game, and the Patriots recovered deep in Chicago territory. New England couldn't move the ball an inch but still went ahead 3–0 on a Tony Franklin field goal. After that, it was all Bears. Led by their dominating, crushing defense and a good offensive performance, it was 46–10 Bears. And once again, the game wasn't as close as the score.

As satisfied as Ditka was, there was one bitter pill. Payton had not scored a touchdown. McMahon had rushed for two touchdowns, Perry had one, and Matt Suhey had one, but Payton did not get his.

Payton was upset about it, and the fact that Payton was upset bothered Ditka. Payton was his favorite player of all time, and Ditka didn't like the idea that his future Hall of Famer was unhappy.

Payton put it behind him and moved on, but it was a flaw in the perfect diamond that was the 1985 season.

Gale Sayers

I love Gale Sayers. He was unbelievable as a football player, and he was a guy I got to see as a teenager in person at Soldier Field. I saw him when he was at his peak, and I have to say that I've never seen anyone better.

That includes the great Walter Payton, Barry Sanders, Emmitt Smith, Eric Dickerson, and any other back you want to name. Of players that I have seen perform either in person or on television, nobody was better than Sayers.

A lot of people will say that Sanders was better than Sayers, but that's just not the case. Sanders had more moves than any five running backs who were playing in the 1990s, and he had a dramatic impact on a team that was basically average (or below) during his career. But just because he was quicker and more elusive than running backs at that time, does that mean he was quicker and more elusive than Sayers?

No it doesn't. Sayers had just as many moves as Sanders, and he was also faster and stronger. So as far as I'm concerned, that's the end of the argument right there. Now there's no reason for anyone to think I'm putting down Sanders for any reason. The guy was one of the best runners of the past 25 years, he's in the Hall of Fame, and he basically carried that team. But if we are talking about Sayers, Sanders was not as good.

Sayers was just a magical player. I have to say that I have always enjoyed talking to him when he has been on the air and that he's a really good guy. I know there are some media people and other radio

Gale Sayers carries the ball in the November 10, 1970, game against the San Francisco 49ers in Chicago. (AP Photo)

guys who may not like Sayers and think he's difficult and aloof, but that's only because they don't know him. Once you get to know Sayers, he's a really good guy and you find that he's really easy to like.

He was a magician when he was running with the ball. He had it all in that he knew when to accelerate and he knew when it was time to slow down. He knew when to make a cut and when not to. He was just so instinctive that he was impossible to stop.

And remember, Sayers did it at a time when the Bears didn't have much of a passing attack. No surprise there. When have the Bears really had a good passing attack since the days of Sid Luckman? The Bears are still waiting for a great quarterback and are simply hoping for decent quarterback play most of the time. But when Payton was playing and at his best, who were the Bears' quarterbacks? Rudy Bukich and Jack Concannon. You won't find them in the Hall of Fame unless they drove to Canton, bought a ticket, and walked around, looking at all the great players there.

Even back then, having a great quarterback took pressure off the running game. It meant that a player wouldn't have to carry the offense on his shoulders. That was not the case with Sayers. He was the guy. He had to do it by himself. Everyone knew he was coming, and he still got the job done better than anybody else who ever played the game.

> "Everyone knew he was coming, and he still got the job done better than anybody else who ever played the game."

I also loved Walter Payton, and there wasn't a thing that he couldn't do on the football field. If you asked me who I would take over the length of his career, I'd have to take Payton. But when you're talking about winning one game when each man was at his absolute best, I have to go with Sayers. He was a lot faster than Walter, and his moves were unbelievable. Payton was more about his punishing style, his tough stiff arm, and his desire to run over you. I don't think anyone would say that Walter was any kind of burner—not even Walter himself.

But Sayers had all the gifts that any running back could hope for. I think Gale has been pretty sensitive about that over the years. He takes it to mean that when somebody says he was talented or had great physical gifts, it means that he wasn't as hard-working as some of the other great running backs. So he resents that kind of talk.

I don't think that's what anyone is saying. Obviously, Sayers did all the work he needed to in order to get to the professional level and then excel at it. But at the same time, he can't say he wasn't extremely talented and that talent allowed him to excel. He doesn't have to apologize for it, either. It almost seems that he feels a little bad because he had more talent and athletic ability than his competition. That doesn't make any sense to me.

Gale had the ability to bide his time before heading upfield. There were times it looked like he was about to get stopped for little or no gain, and then he would find the opening and turn a 2-yard gain into a 50-yarder. That's what separated him from many of the other great backs of the era. Paul Hornung couldn't do that with the Packers and neither could Jim Taylor. Jim Brown? Maybe he could have, but not in the same style. He might run over two or three guys instead of running around them. With Sayers, once he got that first step upfield and he could accelerate, he could fake guys out of position so easily that they wouldn't be able to put their hands on him. That's what made him the great back he was.

I've gotten to know him very well over the years, and he's a really good guy who is genuine and caring. He may protect himself from people he doesn't know well, but so do a lot of people. And when Gale does know you and he lets his guard down, it's obvious what a good guy he really is.

Walter Payton

He was funny and always ready to play a joke. He had a quick wit and really enjoyed being around people. As great a player as Walter Payton was, he was that good a guy.

We used to have him on the radio show, and he could be pretty evasive because he enjoyed playing the media game. He'd make you work for answers because that's how he liked to have fun. When he was on with Dan Jiggetts and me, it was always a highlight, and it was great for us and the station. And it was good for Payton, as well.

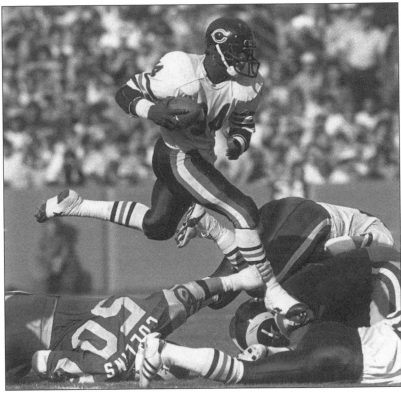

Walter Payton leaps over Los Angeles Rams linebacker Jim Collins (50) during first-half action in Anaheim, California, on November 11, 1984. (AP Photo/Reed Saxon)

We stayed close over the years, and I know I was one of the first ones to realize how sick he was. He was always wearing those sunglasses, and one time he had them off for a few minutes and I saw how yellow his eyes were. He told me he was sick, and he had a few things going on, but I didn't know exactly what it was. You didn't have to be a doctor to know that it was serious. When you saw how the color of his eyes had changed, you knew it was serious. He admitted that it was a big concern in an off-the-air conversation, but again, I didn't know all the details until he chose to reveal them.

When he got sick and later died, it was horrible to lose such a young and great guy. He meant so much to so many people. Above all, people remember him as such an outstanding football player. The numbers were amazing because he broke Jim Brown's record, and he was the guy who was going to get 100 yards every week. When the Bears became a good team, he was the focal point of the offense. The Bears had a great defense, but they had an offensive identity and that was due to Payton and Jim McMahon. I think Walter could really smell how close the Bears were getting during the championship year, and he wasn't going to let that opportunity slip away. You combine him with McMahon, and that's why that offense did so well that year—neither of those players would let that opportunity slip away.

Payton played for so many years with the same ferocity and attitude even when the Bears were average or much worse than that. He ran like he was the best player in football, and he may have been. I've seen guys who were more talented, but I've never seen guys get more out of their talent. He got everything he had out of his ability, and you always realized that Walter was going to hurt people when he ran with the ball.

Instead of getting hit when he ran with it, he was hitting the linebackers who tried to tackle him. He had that stiff arm, and he had so much power. He ran with that high-stepping motion, and he could punish anyone who tried to tackle him.

"I've seen guys who were more talented, but I've never seen guys get more out of their talent."

Everybody made a lot out of Payton as a practical joker. He liked people to laugh, and he liked them to have a good time, but he also loved the shock value. I think that was a big part of why he had that kind of personality.

It was such a shock to see him get sick and die so suddenly. You think about how little time he had after football, and you just felt so awful for his family. But there is no doubt he was the kind of guy who got every minute he could out of life. He may have deserved more time and it's a shame that he died so young, but he got the most he could out of the time he had, and he probably lived more in his 45 years than most people do in 75 or 85 years.

He was a great person and a great football player. His records may have fallen, but Walter Payton was the best all-around running back I ever saw.

Jim McMahon

He was the right quarterback for that team. The 1985 Bears were as good for that one season as any team that has ever played the game, and I think Jim McMahon had as much to do with it as anybody else. I know that this was a team that was dominated by the defense. They were a great defense, and they absolutely killed people. But don't let anyone tell you that it was a one-dimensional team that didn't get anything from the offense. That wasn't true then, and it isn't true now. Don't let anyone revise history on you.

The Bears got plenty of big plays and contributions from the offense, and McMahon was the perfect quarterback. He was a fearless guy on the field. That fearlessness didn't stop him from getting

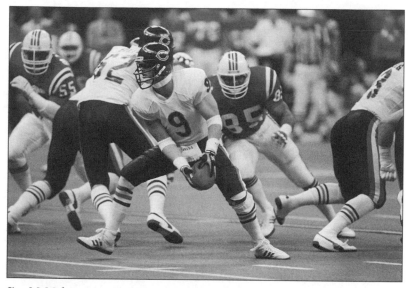

Jim McMahon in action against New England during Super Bowl XX in New Orleans on January 26, 1986. (AP Photo)

hurt a lot on the field or acting like a jerk sometimes off of it. What he did to that West Coast writer (T.J. Simers of the *Los Angeles Times*) was unbelievable. He snotted on him. If he did that to me, he would have had a fight on his hands. I don't know how it would have turned out, but I would have gone down swinging. It's an absolutely sickening and disgusting thing to do to another human being.

Despite the antics, he was some kind of quarterback for the Bears—maybe the ideal quarterback for that team. McMahon's most memorable contribution was coming in that Thursday night game against the Vikings. It was the beginning of the season, and the Bears had won their first couple of games, but he's out against the Vikings and the Bears were behind. McMahon couldn't take it and told Mike Ditka that he's going into the game. Nobody told Ditka anything, but that's just what McMahon did. Ditka let him go in, and he threw this unbelievable touchdown pass to Willie Gault. It was perfect: high-arcing and deep down the far sidelines. Gault just ran under it, and you knew right then and there that the Bears had turned the tide and that they were going to win the game. You also knew that they had a very special team, maybe one that was as good as any that had been seen for a long time.

There were some great quarterbacks at the time, like Joe Montana with the 49ers and Dan Marino with the Dolphins. But was there anyone who was any better for that Bears team than McMahon? I don't think so. Remember, he was not just some guy the Bears had stuck in there at quarterback. He was first-round draft choice from Brigham Young, and he had his name all over the BYU record book. BYU was a quarterback team, and McMahon was the one who set records. He could play the game, and he knew the game. He could really dominate when he had to.

Look at Montana—he was a third-round draft pick from Notre Dame. He happened to get with the right coach in Bill Walsh, who knew just what he was doing with quarterbacks. Walsh won with Montana, and he got Steve Young going in the right direction when he came from Tampa Bay. The fact that Young won a Super Bowl when George Seifert was head coach doesn't matter, as far as I'm concerned. He became a great quarterback because he learned from Walsh.

My point is: how good do you think Montana would have been had he been drafted by the New Orleans Saints or the Atlanta Falcons? He would have been this third-round guy from Notre Dame you might never have heard of again. Look what happened to Young when he was with Tampa Bay. He got absolutely destroyed and was thrown around like a rag doll because it was an awful team that could not protect the quarterback. He came to San Francisco and he was a star, maybe the best quarterback in the game when he won his Super Bowl, and he became a Hall of Famer. What do you think would have happened to Montana if he had been on the same team that Young had been on in Tampa? He would have been killed. Montana was not a big guy. He was small, and while he could run, he couldn't run like Fran Tarkenton. So you would have never remembered Montana had he been on that team. He would have been just another quarterback who got beat up because he played for a lousy team.

That's one of the reasons I like Terry Bradshaw so much as a quarterback. He was drafted by the Steelers with the No. 1 pick—after winning a coin toss with the Bears and getting that No. 1 pick—and Pittsburgh was just an awful team. How bad were the Steelers and how tough was it for Bradshaw early on? That's why I admire him so much. He had to take so much abuse early on and he took it, hung in there, and became a great one.

I don't think Bradshaw gets anywhere near the credit he should. He played on a team that became one of the all-time best, and just look at the talent around him. The defensive guys were great, with Joe Greene, Jack Lambert, Mel Blount, Dwight White, and Jack Ham. I mean that whole defensive team was awesome.

But they had the quality guys on offense, as well. Lynn Swann and John Stallworth. That's some pair of receivers to have, and then you have Franco Harris in the backfield. That's awesome talent. Bradshaw didn't have Bill Walsh working with him to get him better. He pretty much improved on his own. He paid his dues and became the kind of quarterback that you wanted out there in any big game. It really doesn't matter in the long run how many touchdown passes you threw and how many yards you had. Those things are all nice, and I'm not saying Marino wasn't a great quarterback because he didn't win a Super Bowl and he only got there once. But a guy like Bradshaw—look how he did when he was in the big games, any playoff game, AFC Championship Game, or Super Bowl. He was at his best in so many of those big games. That's why I would take him as my No. 1 quarterback of all time. He was up against so many great teams, and it didn't bother him—it brought out the best in him.

And that brings me back to McMahon. He had a lot of the same qualities and characteristics that Bradshaw had. It's wasn't his fault he got hurt. You can call him injury-prone and say that those injuries kept him from becoming what he could have been. But you can also look at what he did when he was healthy and look at the way he played. It was all about winning and getting the most out of himself and his teammates.

McMahon had a strong personality for the Bears, and that's just what they needed from him. Look at the defense they had with all that talent. It could have been like so many Bears teams we have seen with the great defense that overwhelms the offense with its personality and strength. But McMahon was not about to let that happen. He was strong. He stood up for his offensive teammates and would not let them get swept aside by an overwhelming defense. He made sure they all got their credit.

I'm not going to go overboard and say that McMahon was one of the best quarterbacks of all time. You can't say that, because he didn't stay healthy and he didn't play long enough for that to happen. But when he was in there and he was at his best, he had many of the qualities that make a quarterback great, and it all happened for him and the Bears in that amazing 1985 season—even if McMahon wasn't fully healthy that year. But he was in the game often enough that his signature was all over that team, and I guarantee you they wouldn't have won like they did without him. Remember, they only lost one game that year, and he didn't play that Monday night game against the Dolphins.

All the talk was that the defense had a bad game, and Marino came up with the perfect game to beat them. That may have been the case, but there were also a number of lucky plays and there was no McMahon. How would the Bears have done in that game if McMahon was playing? They might have won that game, and the Bears might have gone undefeated. It would have been a beautiful thing.

GREATEST QUARTERBACKS

Here are the five best quarterbacks who have played in the NFL. These are not the names you will see on a lot of the lists that are done by the so-called experts. These are the guys who I would have on my team if I was building a franchise.

1. TERRY BRADSHAW, PITTSBURGH

He was simply the guy I would want on the field for any big game that my team had to have. He had it all, and he had to take a lot of crap for being dumb. Hollywood Henderson trashed this guy and said he couldn't spell "cat" if you spotted him the "c" and the "a." Well, we all should be so dumb as Bradshaw. If he's so dumb, why is he still making money in football as the lead guy on the Fox pregame show 25 years after he last played in the NFL?

But none of that newspaper talk had anything to do with the way he played. He was tough, man. He could hang in the pocket, scramble out of trouble, make plays with his legs, or make a big throw with his arm. He was big enough and strong enough to take a brutal hit and come back and make another big throw the next play without having to come out of the game. Four championships clinch it for me. I am not going to rate every quarterback based on the number of championships because it doesn't always tell the story. But in Bradshaw's case it really does, because his team was so awful before he got there. Once he learned the ropes, the Steelers started winning championships. You go ahead and take Montana, Marino, or Peyton Manning. I'm taking Bradshaw, and I like my chances.

2. OTTO GRAHAM, CLEVELAND

I think a lot of the quarterbacks from pro football's past get completely forgotten, and that just isn't right. People don't know who Otto Graham is or what he did that was so fantastic. But I am not going to let him be forgotten or lumped in with a bunch of other guys because he played before every game was aired on television.

The Cleveland Browns came into the NFL as basically an expansion team. There was another league called All-America Football Conference, and Cleveland was playing in that league and they were absorbed by the NFL (along with the San Francisco 49ers and Baltimore Colts). The Browns came into the league, and in their first game they absolutely destroyed the defending NFL champion Philadelphia Eagles and went on to win the title in their first year. Graham led the Browns to 10 division or league titles in 10 years. You can't argue with that.

3. Fran Tarkenton, Minnesota–New York Giants

Just about everybody on this list has won Super Bowl titles and NFL Championships and done it multiple times—everyone except Tarkenton. No, he didn't win one Super Bowl, but I am not going to hold it against him. This guy came into the league with everything working against him, and all he ever did was fire the football downfield and become a dominant quarterback even though he was small and everybody said he couldn't do it. His own coach, Norm Van Brocklin, couldn't stand him. Van Brocklin was an old-school quarterback and he didn't like how Tarkenton would scramble around and run or buy time and make a late throw. Yeah, he didn't like it because he couldn't do it. There was jealousy there.

Tarkenton came in as a rookie on an expansion team and beat the Bears in their first game. He was awesome. He didn't have a huge arm, but he could make every throw and he did it with receivers like Paul Flatley and guys who were only average. He left the Vikings and went to the worst Giants team you could imagine and he made them competitive. He came back to Minnesota and played in three Super Bowls. He didn't win any of them and really didn't play well in any of them, but he was as great a quarterback as you could imagine.

Tarkenton was as productive as he could be, but he was also an innovator. He basically invented a new way for the position of quarterback to be played. Before Fran came along, there was no such thing as a scrambling quarterback. You were supposed to sit in the pocket, step up, and throw the ball. If you had to take your shot, you did it. Start running around to get out of trouble? Nobody did that before Tarkenton.

Now teams want their quarterbacks to have mobility and be able to buy time by moving away from the pressure and running if they have to. I think all quarterbacks owe Tarkenton a debt of gratitude for creating that style of play. And it's not like it was widely accepted, either. People looked at him and asked why he was running around. "What's he trying to prove?" they would ask.

Well, he wasn't trying to prove anything. He was just trying to make a play and help his team win the game. You get questions when a guy is an innovator and he doesn't fit the mold of what you think a star quarterback is supposed to look like. And so many of those questions came from his own coach. Can you imagine being the main guy in a company and having the president question you every step of the way? That's what it was like for Tarkenton. Even with all that, he still became one of the greatest quarterbacks of all time, and that's why you have to admire him so much.

And he was up against some of the best defensive players the game has ever seen. He was scrambling away from pressure and keeping his eyes on the downfield receivers trying to make a play as he was trying to get away from Bob Lilly, Deacon Jones, and Dick Butkus. These were guys who would kill the quarterback when they got their hands on him, and this was at a time when there were no rules protecting the quarterback.

Tarkenton neutralized the top defensive players of the day. Do you think Deacon Jones worried about going up against any other quarterback? No way in the world. He was a great pass rusher who only wanted to intimidate quarterbacks. He knew he couldn't do that with Tarkenton because he could run away from him and not just run out of bounds. He would run for yardage or run to buy time and make a play. At the end of the game, Tarkenton was still standing, and the pass rushers were the ones with their hands on their sides looking for a little air.

4. Joe Montana, San Francisco

I'm not the biggest Montana fan, but you do have to give credit to a quarterback who won four Super Bowls. Has any other quarterback won four? Just Terry Bradshaw. That's quite a twosome.

I think you have to give an awful lot of credit to Bill Walsh, and Montana knows he has to thank the good Lord above that he ended up in San Francisco. Here's a guy who knew more about offense than anyone, and luckily for a guy like Montana, Walsh was able to teach what he knew very well to his student.

That's not a putdown of Montana because I don't think Walsh would have been as successful with too many other quarterbacks at the helm. They couldn't have learned the lessons the way Montana did. There's no doubt that Montana simply had great touch when he threw the ball. How many times did Jerry Rice have to reach back for the ball or how many times did Dwight Clark have to dive for one of Montana's passes? Not many. Nearly everything he threw was right in stride.

Okay, Clark did have to go up and get one particular pass in the corner of the end zone when the 49ers were playing the Cowboys in the NFC Championship Game. That only became one of the most famous plays in NFL history because Clark seemingly climbed a 12-foot ladder to go get it. But it's not like it was a bad pass. All Montana did was put the ball in a spot where Clark could get it and Cowboy cornerback Everson Walls could only watch. That's what being a good quarterback is all about.

So I give credit to Montana for being a great one. But I can't give him too much credit. Ask yourself if Montana would have been the great player and Hall of Famer he turned out to be if he had been drafted by the Atlanta Falcons or the New Orleans Saints. Do you think he would have had the same success under a coach named Leeman Bennett? I don't think so, and I don't think it would have been close.

Yes, Montana was still a good quarterback after he left the 49ers and went to Kansas City. But that's all he was—good. He was no longer great and a guy who could take over the game every single week and do everything he wanted.

Further proof is the case of Steve Young. Look at the numbers he put up and the records he set when he was in his prime with the 49ers. He has the highest passer rating in the history of football. But just where was he before he got to the 49ers? He was getting his ass kicked in Tampa, and he was clueless on the football field. He was one of those guys who was always trying to do too much, and he looked like a chicken with his head cut off.

Then Young worked with Walsh and Montana and when he got his turn, he finally became a great quarterback. He learned from one of the greatest teachers of all time and a great first-string quarterback in Montana. And in Montana's case, he learned from a great teacher.

I think Montana was great, but I don't think he was No. 1.

5. Sid Luckman, Chicago

I don't think there are too many people who have watched football that would still have Luckman on their list of all-time great quarterbacks. The guys from that era are just about forgotten. But you can't leave that guy off because he played in the 1940s (1939–1950). First of all, his name is still all over the Bears record book. A guy who played back then still holds records for a team, and it's nearly 60 years after he last put on a uniform.

Not only was he a great passer, he did it with a ball that was shaped more like a basketball than one of today's footballs.

It's also a pretty good indictment of what kind of quarterbacks the Bears have had over the years that many of Luckman's records from a 10-, 11-, or 12-game season are still standing today. But that's the truth. They've had a lot of guys who were bad, a lot of guys who were average, and some who were good. But when it comes to having great quarterbacks, the Bears just haven't had them very often.

Dave Wannstedt

Without a doubt, the saddest chapter of Chicago Bears history was written when Dave Wannstedt was head coach. There were Bears teams with worse records and there were Bears teams that made just as many mistakes, but the Wannstedt era was all about incompetence, self pity, and making excuses.

None of this had anything to do with Bears football, neither the kind we grew up watching with George Halas on the sidelines nor the Super Bowl Bears of 1985. The Bears had teams that ranged from awful to dominating, but they were respected. They were respected

The Wannstedt era was all about incompetence, self pity, and making excuses. Here, NFL official Red Cashion, left, is shown talking to Chicago Bears head coach Dave Wannstedt, during the Bears-Broncos game in Denver on Sunday, November 10, 1996. (AP Photo)

because they played with fire and played with toughness. If the Bears weren't good enough to beat you, you were at least going to come out of that game knowing that you had been in a street fight. Nasty and hard-hitting, the Bears would at least hit you back if they were getting run over during a game. They wouldn't just accept it blindly.

After Halas, some coaches had the same kind of mentality and some didn't. Ditka had the chip on his shoulder and knew how to challenge his players. He was all about emotion and toughness and demanding the best performance he could get. Of course, he was also about getting commercials and endorsements, but that really had nothing to do with the kind of coach he was—or the kind of player he was, for that matter. He demanded a lot of himself, and he demanded a lot from his players.

When it all fell apart for Ditka and he was fired after the 1992 season, it was the beginning of a new era in football, not just for the Bears but in all of football. The Steelers had hired Bill Cowher the year before, and the Bears wanted to get that hot, young assistant coach on the rise. What better place to go in order to find that assistant than the Super Bowl? The Cowboys were playing the Bills in the Super Bowl, and Jimmy Johnson's right-hand man in Dallas was Wannstedt. He was in charge of that defense, and the Cowboys were big favorites in that game during Super Bowl week. As the media was looking for stories, they had hooked on to Wannstedt as that year's hot assistant. He was the defensive coordinator of the team that was about to win the Super Bowl, so he was the anointed one.

But did anyone actually listen to anything he said? Was there anything about Dave Wannstedt that indicated he would be a legitimate head coach? There was nothing. From the minute I first saw him and from the minute I first heard him, there was nothing there that told me he should be the head coach of the Bears.

I wasn't trying to be mean, and I wasn't trying to be nasty. It's just the way I saw it. I have been wrong before, and I have admitted it.

But I was the first one to start hammering away at Wannstedt, and eventually everyone jumped on board. I was right. He was coach of the Bears for six years, and while they made the playoffs once in that span, they never really had a chance. Wannstedt was simply in way over his head from the start. This was not a guy you could follow into battle. He didn't have that kind of personality or leadership himself. He seemed like a guy who was just flying by the seat of his pants and really didn't know what he was doing.

> "Was there anything about Dave Wannstedt that indicated he would be a legitimate head coach?"

The biggest problem with Wannstedt was that he couldn't see more than one step ahead at any point. When you're coaching in the NFL, you are supposed to see two, three, or four steps ahead, and you're supposed to know what you're talking about. Wannstedt couldn't see more than one step ahead, and he was wrong about almost everything.

Then came the excuses. He always seemed to have some kind of reason when the Bears lost, and none of those reasons had anything to do with his coaching when the Bears lost. "We were just two or three plays away from winning the game. Aaap," Wannstedt would say. That was his mantra. Yeah, two or three plays away from winning the game if you could have stopped a 50-yard touchdown, a 60-yard touchdown and you could have scored one more touchdown yourself.

Remarks like those used to go unchallenged. Wannstedt could say anything and the media would eat it up because he was a friendly guy who would answer questions and fill up notebooks and tape recorders. As a result, the guy got a pass for years.

But that didn't change what we knew at the time. He was not a good NFL coach. He didn't lead, and he didn't make good decisions. Other than that, he did just fine.

The rest of the world finally came around in Wannstedt's last couple of years when it became obvious the team was lost and that he couldn't control players like Bryan Cox and Alonzo Spellman. The overall Wannstedt chapter was a very sad one for this team, although it gave us plenty to talk about on the air over the years.

Brian Urlacher

I am never going to say Urlacher is not a very good player. But there's no way I'm going to put him in a category with Mike Singletary and especially Dick Butkus. Both Singletary and Butkus would leave everything they have on the field to make a tackle.

Can you say the same thing about Urlacher? No way.

Singletary was a great player, but Butkus ranks with the greatest NFL players of all time at any position, not just middle linebacker. I saw Butkus play even though his knees were destroyed, and he still dominated games. He was the rare player who didn't try to save himself or just make a play. He wanted to kill the guy on the other side of the line of scrimmage, and I think he was the kind of player who had opponents scared most of the time.

You talk to anybody who played with him or played against him and they will tell you the same thing. Butkus was the kind of player who gave everything he had on every play. He didn't just want to make a tackle—he wanted to grind his opponent into the turf. He could play the pass, he could play the run, and he could get after the quarterback.

He may not have been that fast when timed with a stopwatch. Ed O'Bradovich said it would take you three days to time Butkus in a running race. But slap the helmet and shoulder pads on him, and it was a completely different story. Then Butkus moved like the wind.

Brian Urlacher (54) leaps to intercept a pass from Carolina Panthers quarterback Jake Delhomme intended for Nick Goings in the second quarter of the NFC divisional playoff game in Chicago on Sunday, January 15, 2006. (AP Photo/Jeff Roberson)

He exploded into the open in order to make tackles. There was no flowing to the ball—he just got right after everyone.

Now that brings us back to Urlacher. He is a good player. But does he do any of the things that Butkus did? Are opponents afraid of Urlacher, and do they fear being on the same field with him? I don't think so. To me, he is another player. He might be pretty good and certainly better than average. But Singletary was the leader of the greatest defense of all time, and Butkus might very well be the best defensive player to ever put on a uniform, so it's not a good comparison.

"Are opponents afraid of Urlacher, and do they fear being on the same field with him?

He's got speed and he can cover a lot of ground, but does he really intimidate people? Do you think opposing running backs or receivers coming over the middle are afraid of him? No. And it's not just a matter of scaring people just to scare them—it's about putting the fear of God in them so they can't do their jobs very well. That's what Singletary did, and that's certainly the way Butkus did it. Urlacher? Not very often, if he does it at all.

The other big difference is how Urlacher plays the run compared to the other two. You used to see Butkus literally throw blockers away from the play until he found the ball carrier so he could bury him. Singletary had Steve McMichael and Dan Hampton in front of him, which was a huge advantage, but he would come busting in and smack people first and ask questions later. They weren't worried about anything but laying out the ball carrier.

Urlacher can't get away from the blocking. When a blocker has him, it takes too much of an effort for him to get away. He makes a few tackles where you're impressed with the hit, but it doesn't happen enough. He doesn't get away from the blockers the same way Butkus and Singletary did.

That's my biggest issue—the consistency factor. Sometimes Urlacher looks as good as anybody, and other times he disappears from view. He'll go one or two series without making a tackle. And that's the thing. They always add tackles to his total after looking at the game films, but to the fans in the stands or Bears fans watching the game on television, we know what's happening. You can't just add numbers to his total and say he was involved in 15, 16, or 17 tackles. We're watching the game.

You shouldn't do that, and you shouldn't have to do it. His totals should stand on their own.

1985 Bears vs. 1963 Bears

They have been the dominant team in Chicago for more than two decades. Despite all the success the Bulls had with Michael Jordan— and I would never belittle any of the six titles that they won—the biggest and best of all the Chicago teams in my lifetime has been the 1985 Bears. They had it all and were one of the best teams the NFL has ever seen.

I wish they would have won more than one Super Bowl. But they didn't. They couldn't sustain their success the way a lot of the great all-time teams do. But as far as Chicago football is concerned, I would take the '85 Bears over the previous champions, the 1963 Bears, by a pretty big margin.

The '85 Bears were a dominant and hungry team, and I think they were better across the board. It's not that the '63 Bears wouldn't have had any advantages and they certainly were deserving champions, but they were not as talented as the '85 team.

Start at quarterback. Who are you going to take? Jim McMahon or Bill Wade? It's no contest. Wade was a nice guy and he got the job done, but McMahon had that special thing inside him to make the big play at the key moment. He was very special and was the perfect leader for this team. That famous Thursday night game at Minnesota in which he came off the bench and started throwing touchdown passes is what made McMahon so special. He was the kind of quarterback who would diagnose what his offense needed to do and figure out what it would take for the Bears to win the game. If they were in a dominant position and could win with their defense and running game, that's what McMahon would do. But if they needed to start throwing the ball, there was no hesitation.

The look McMahon had was one that said, "I'll do whatever it takes to win this game." That's what happened in the Minnesota game and at other points throughout the season. He may not have had huge numbers, but he made big plays.

Wade was a nice quarterback who was not going to hurt the Bears. Talk about managing the game. That's just how George Halas played back then. He didn't want his quarterbacks making mistakes and giving the opposition chances to get back in the game. I remember Wade being a guy who could throw a good pass, but he was no Johnny Unitas or Bart Starr. He was good but not great, and I have to give McMahon a pretty big edge.

Okay, it was a clear-cut win for McMahon over Wade, but how do you call it at the running back position? Walter Payton vs. Joe Marconi. Joe Marconi? Yes, you can look it up. The fullback was the leading rusher for the Bears in 1962 and '63, and he was a nice, hard-trying player. But you know what? He wasn't any kind of star. He didn't even hit 500 yards for the Bears (446 yards) and still led the team. Are you kidding me? They also had Ronnie Bull, Willie Galimore, and Rick Casares to give them a little bit of diversity, but it was still a no-contest battle. All Payton all day.

Payton would get as many yards in one game as Marconi got in about three games—two games if he really was on fire. Payton was the best all-around running back the Bears ever had, and he may have been the best ever as far as being an all-around player in NFL history. Payton was on fire that year. He ran the ball great, he blocked like a madman, and he could catch passes and even throw when Mike Ditka asked him to. You know what I remember? The Bears lost to Miami in that Monday night game, which kept them from going undefeated. Then they came home and beat a bad Colts team and were anything but impressive. The Bears won by a touchdown, and then they went on the road against a Jets team that was fighting for the playoffs.

The Bears weren't fighting for anything. They couldn't go unde-feated anymore, and they were already the top team in the NFC. But they went to the Meadowlands and played a tough game against a team that really needed a win. It was mostly the defense that won the game, but the offense came from Payton running the ball. He ran it even though the Jets defense knew he was coming, and they still couldn't stop him.

That's because Walter knew what the season was all about. He knew that the Bears were all about greatness that year and that he had to leave everything on the field in every game. He did it in that game, and he did it all season. You could have 10 Joe Marconis and it wouldn't be the same as having one Walter Payton. No disrespect intended.

"You could have 10 Joe Marconis and it wouldn't be the same as having one Walter Payton."

And then throw in a fullback like Matt Suhey. It just gave the '85 Bears one more edge. Suhey was some blocker, and when he had the chance to run the ball, he made it count.

Let's take a look at the wide receivers. The Bears have never had overly impressive wideouts and that includes the '85 team. Willie

Gault had the speed and the flash, but did he have the consistency? I don't think so. Dennis McKinnon was a hard-working guy and was good at his job. But was he a great receiver? I don't think you can say that. But what I will say is that when the Bears decided to go to him, he was up to making a play in a big situation. Dennis Gentry and Emery Moorehead were also tough receivers who McMahon could count on. It was a nice group, and they got the job done. But the Bears weren't exactly the San Francisco 49ers or the Miami Dolphins with Dan Marino. They did not throw the ball around very much. It was not about the passing game. But you have to give the '85 Bears a passing grade for their receivers. They made big plays and they did well in the clutch. They just didn't have huge numbers.

In 1963, the Bears weren't exactly a wild offensive team, either. They were as conservative as you could be for a championship team. But like the '85 team, they made plays in the clutch. And they had two stars among their receivers—Johnny Morris and, of course, Mike Ditka. You know, Ditka was famous for running people over, and there's that one highlight play they used to show back from that 1963 season when I think he ran over, past, or through nine guys on the Steelers. He was a very talented tight end, and he led the Bears in receptions. Morris was second.

Ditka was the best tight end that the Bears have ever had. That may seem obvious because they've had so many seasons when the tight end wasn't even a factor. But when Ditka was playing for the Bears and Halas, the old man liked his heart and his passion and was not afraid to throw to him under any situation.

Then you have Morris. He may not have been the fastest receiver, but he ran very good routes and the guy knew how to get open. And if he could get his hands on the ball, he would catch it. He was the definition of dependable.

I'd be willing to say the 1963 Bears were even with the '85 team in the pass-catching department. Maybe I'm being generous, and maybe you could make an argument to give the '85 Bears the edge. But the '63 Bears had a great tight end who could go get it in every situation and make a play. Ditka was a star back then, and he was tremendous in 1963. I don't think the '85 Bears had any star wide receivers.

Now let's take a look at the offensive lines. The 1963 Bears had a good line, and they worked hard and won most of the battles, but the 1985 Bears had one of the best offensive lines that ever played the game. Not just among Bears teams, either. Overall, that group with Jim Covert and Keith Van Horne as the two tackles, Tom Thayer and Mark Bortz as guards, and Jay Hilgenberg in the middle was outstanding. Those guys were just dominant blockers.

You know everyone talks about Covert and Hilgenberg. I think those two got the most notoriety, and they were sensational players. But Thayer and Bortz were really good players who did everything right that year. Those two guys were very aggressive, and I think a lot of the Bears' swagger came from the offensive line that year. It's obvious how good the defense was, but you need a complete team to win a championship, and the Bears' offensive line gave them an edge on the offensive side of the ball.

If you don't think those guys were special, then you don't know football. McMahon used to hang out with his offensive linemen because he knew how good they were and how important they were to the team's all-around success. Payton knew how good his offensive line was, and he really appreciated them. They fed off of him, and he fed off of them.

The 1963 Bears had a good offensive line. I'm not taking anything away from those guys. They had Mike Pyle at center, and he was solid. Ted Karras was a good left guard. I would say those were the two best blockers that year. Throw in Bob Wetoska, Roger Davis, and Herman Lee (okay, I had to look them up), and you had a pretty good unit.

The last time I checked, pretty good does not compare to great. I don't think you would find too many people who would disagree, including those '63 Bears. The 1985 offensive line was great in every facet of the game, and they were better than their fellow offensive linemen from the 1963 team. Period. Exclamation point. End of story.

Defense rules the day.

"If you don't think those guys were special, then you don't know football."

In many ways, both teams were similar in their makeup. Both were championship teams that had good offenses and dominant defenses. That's the way the Bears played the game when George Halas was on the sideline throwing nickels around like manhole covers (Mike Ditka's great line), and that's the way they have been all the way through the Lovie Smith era.

It's doubtful there has been any team in the history of football that played the game any better on the defensive side of the ball than the Bears did in 1985. I'm not saying they were the best defensive team ever. I wouldn't say that because they only won the one title. But that particular season, the Bears played as well defensively as the best Steelers teams, the best Green Bay teams under Vince Lombardi, or the best Miami Dolphin teams, including the one that went undefeated.

The only team you could compare them with was the great Steelers' teams. I don't know that the Packers or Dolphins defenses ever inspired the fear that the '85 Bears did. People were afraid when they had to play the Steelers, but they fell down to their knees and started shaking when they had to play the Bears.

Start off with the defensive line. Richard Dent was as good a pass rusher as there was at the time. He was a perfect fit for that team because he was a great athlete who would find a way to get to the quarterback. That was his job because Steve McMichael, Dan

Defense rules the day. Here, Richard Dent chases a loose ball during the NFL playoffs on January 16, 1986. (AP Photo)

Hampton, and the Fridge were right there next to him. Hampton was a great Hall of Fame player who could go anywhere on the defensive line and make a play and fit right in. I think he was the best all-around football player on the team. I mean, the guy is in the Hall of Fame, for crying out loud. It has to stand for something.

I think people tend to forget how good McMichael was. Everybody remembers him for all his antics on TV with his little dog and for all the pro wrestling stuff. But he was a great football player who gave the Bears everything he had. He was tough on the field and did everything he could to win the battle so the Bears would win the game. I would call him an honest football player. He may have been working any angle he could find outside the game to make money—and who can blame him for that—but on the field, he was a stand-up guy who went out and made the play.

William Perry wasn't the same kind of player as those other guys, but the Fridge was special. You know Ditka loved him, and he especially loved using him as a weapon out of the backfield on offense. On defense, he had his moments. I'll never forget that play he made against Detroit in the last game of the 1985 regular season. He picked up a fumble on the run and off he rumbled downfield. I know he didn't make it all the way to the end zone, but it was great to watch him pick it up and run before he ran out of gas.

Buddy Ryan didn't like him. Buddy Ryan didn't like any rookies. But that didn't mean that Perry couldn't play because he really could. He didn't have a long run with the Bears because he ate so much and he got so fat, but he was fun to watch that season—there's no doubt about it.

I would say the defensive line may have been the strongest part of the 1963 Bears, as well. Doug Atkins and OB (Ed O'Bradovich) were the defensive ends. That's a pretty nice pair to draw to. OB was just a great player, solid against the run, and he could really get after the quarterback. I know he didn't like having to chase down Fran Tarkenton, but he could catch the other quarterbacks.

Then you have Atkins. He was just a mean, nasty, ornery, and very strong guy who was simply a dominant player. Nobody could stop him when he was on top of his game. The Bears front four didn't have a nickname like the Purple People Eaters (Minnesota Vikings) or the Fearsome Foursome (L.A. Rams), but if they had, people might still know them today. Even without a nickname, they still get a lot of respect here in Chicago, but I don't know many people outside of this area who give them the credit they deserve.

And it wasn't just Atkins and OB. Earl Leggett and Stan Jones were the tackles. Not fancy players, but they were good, solid guys who didn't make mistakes.

The '63 Bears had some great linebackers. Remember, Dick Butkus, the greatest defensive player who ever played football, wouldn't be drafted for two more years. But it's not like they didn't have a middle linebacker. They had Bill George who set the standard that Butkus had to live up to. They also had Joe Fortunato and Larry Morris as the two outside guys.

George might have been every bit the equal of Mike Singletary for the 1985 Bears. He might have even been a little bit better. Singletary was a great student of the game and a very good player. But he had Hampton and McMichael playing in front of him, and he didn't have offensive lineman getting clean shots at him very often. That's a big factor.

I would say George might get a small edge over Singletary. The guy was just a great middle linebacker. He was all over the field, and he didn't have the benefit of having Hall of Fame defensive linemen in front of him.

But you have to give the '85 Bears the overall edge at linebacker with Otis Wilson and Wilber Marshall. Wilson was not the greatest technician, and I always got the feeling that he was doing pretty much what he wanted and not necessarily what was best for the overall defense. I know he couldn't really get away with that kind of freelancing playing for Ryan, but there were times you could tell he didn't follow through on his assignment the way Ryan wanted him to. But when he got after the passer or dropped into coverage, his speed was amazing.

Yet the key player to that whole defense was Marshall. I'm not saying he was the best player because I don't think anyone was better than Hampton. But Marshall was this frightening guy who scared the opposition. You could see the steam coming off of him, and he just wanted to hurt somebody before he came off the field. When the Bears took apart the Patriots in the Super Bowl, it was Marshall who frightened them. I think Tony Eason is still cleaning up the mess he made in that game, and the same goes for Steve Grogan. They were absolutely scared out of their minds at the Bears' defense in general and Marshall in particular.

"The key player to that whole defense was Marshall."

The secondary is the one area on the 1985 Bears that you could pick on a little bit. Not really because they brought so much pressure with the guys up front. Mike Richardson was an average cornerback, and if he had been playing on a team that couldn't get to the quarterback the way the Bears could, he would have been exposed as such. I think the Bears knew that he was a bit of a liability back there, but what could you do? They had All-Pro guys just about everywhere else on defense so you can have one position where you are just average. Leslie Frazier was a very good cover guy, and it's too bad he got hurt in the Super Bowl.

Gary Fencik and Dave Duerson were big hitters playing at free safety and strong safety. You remember that they had Todd Bell the year before in Duerson's position, and he was really nasty. Bell picked the wrong year to hold out, and Duerson took advantage of it.

Richie Petitbon and Rosey Taylor were two great safeties on the '63 Bears. They might have been just as good as Fencik and Duerson. Taylor knew where the ball was and he knew where it was going to be. He just went and got it. Petitbon covered like a cornerback, as well, and he was a good hitter. Dave Whitsell and Bennie McRae lined up at cornerback for the 1963 team, and they don't have to take a backseat to the '85 guys. Whitsell was a ball hawk, and McRae was a great cover guy, as well. I'll give the '63 Bears an edge in the secondary.

So if you add it all up, the '63 Bears get the check mark for their defensive backs, and they are even as far as the receivers go. But in every other area, the '85 Bears get the edge, and some of those advantages are big.

We didn't even talk about the coaching. George Halas vs. Mike Ditka. Ahh, we don't have to talk about that one because we're letting the players do the playing. But if we did talk about the coaching, we'd give the edge to Ditka. The Old Man was coming to the end of his reign by that time, while Ditka was at the top of the game.

The '85 Bears would have won a game between the two teams, and even though I love that '63 team, I don't think it would have been very close.

State of the Bears

The Bears are an agonizing team. They make the Super Bowl in 2006 and miss the playoffs for the next two years. They swing and miss on first-round draft picks, yet the general manager talks about finding a quarterback who can dominate a game and take the Bears to the next level.

If I really look at the team from the Super Bowl year and the next two seasons, I come to certain conclusions. First of all, Lovie Smith is a good coach. He may not be a good quote, and he may be the last guy you want to have on a talk show, but that doesn't matter at all. He knows how to coach players, and they want to play for him.

He knows what he is doing, too. If you look at the team that went to the Super Bowl, it wasn't exactly overflowing with talent. And in the 2008 season, I think he got everything out of the team that he could. If you think about what people were saying before the start of the season, it was not supposed to be a very good year. I think most of the so-called Bears experts were saying that this was going to be a losing team. The most optimistic prediction was that if everything went well, they might be at .500 or within a game of it.

Instead, you had a team with a winning record that was playing for a spot in the playoffs in the last game of the season. That tells me that

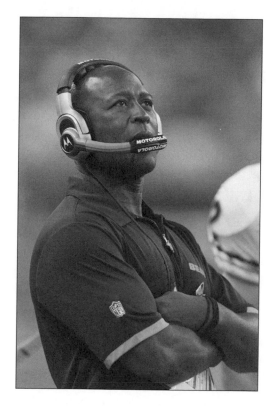

Lovie Smith is a good coach. Here he watches from the sidelines against the Detroit Lions in the fourth quarter of a game in Detroit, Michigan, on Sunday, October 5, 2008. (AP Photo/Paul Sancya)

you really have a coach who can get the most out of the talent that he has. So I don't have a problem with Lovie Smith. The Bears have a good coach, and he is getting whatever his players have to give.

But that's not the whole story with this team. I don't like the way Jerry Angelo is running this team, and I don't like the way he is thinking about this team. He is not giving Smith the weapons he needs to work with. In a lot of cases, Angelo is making things worse.

There are a lot of examples, but let's start with Matt Forte. I like Forte. I think he is a good running back. No doubt that he had a productive rookie year. But I don't think you can say he is going to be another Gale Sayers or another Walter Payton. I don't think you can say he is going to be another Thomas Jones, either.

"I don't like the way Jerry Angelo is running this team, and I don't like the way he is thinking about this team."

That's the problem. The Bears picked Forte in the second round and he gave them excellent production in his rookie season. But remember, it was just a few years ago that Angelo was picking Cedric Benson to be the No. 1 running back. That pick turned out to be a disaster. Benson was nothing but a baby with the Bears, and he was the last thing you want your running back to be. Even though Benson was a disaster, the Bears still had Jones, and he did a great job of running the ball. So good that he helped the Bears get to the Super Bowl in 2006.

So at the end of that off-season, Angelo decided to let Jones go and give the starting position to Benson who didn't deserve it and probably didn't even want it. At least that's how I looked at it. I looked at Cedric Benson and I saw somebody who didn't care very much about what he was doing on the football field. If he did care, he sure had a strange way of showing it. He didn't run very hard—he didn't run anything like a No. 1 draft pick is supposed to.

To me, that's on Jerry Angelo. He's supposed to be such a student of the game and know so much about the draft. But it's a joke with what has happened with the players that he has taken in the first round through the years. You have Chris Williams in 2008, and the guy had a bad back. You can spin it any way you want, but he was not on the field as a rookie. You can say it takes time for a player to develop, but the Falcons had a rookie quarterback in Matt Ryan playing *every* game. So did the Ravens with Joe Flacco. The Bears couldn't pick a healthy player? Give me a break.

Just look at some of the other No. 1 draft picks under Angelo. Marc Colombo? I guess he's doing pretty well for Dallas, but he couldn't get on the field here because he was hurt. Michael Haynes at defensive end? The guy from Penn State? He couldn't play dead. Tommie Harris is okay and so is Greg Olsen, but this is not a stellar record. You have to wonder if this guy has any idea of what he's doing.

You know what really bothers me about Angelo? At the end of the season, he's giving his end-of-the-year analysis and he's saying the Bears have to look long and hard at the quarterback position. How it all begins and ends with the quarterback.

It's like he's saying that it's Kyle Orton's fault the Bears weren't in the playoffs. The fact of the matter is that the Bears wouldn't have been as close as they were to getting into the playoffs if it weren't for Orton. He gave them everything he had, and he was good. Now, he wasn't as good after he hurt his foot as he was before, and it seems like Angelo is holding that foot injury against Orton. You can't do that.

It's not about getting a new quarterback in here. I'm not saying the Bears wouldn't want a great one like John Elway or Steve Young or a young Dan Marino, but you just don't find guys like that. The Bears have a competent quarterback in Orton. What the Bears need to do is get him some competent wide receivers.

I'm not saying Bernard Berrian is a Hall of Famer or anything close. But he is a competent and fast wideout who made Minnesota a better team, and the fact that he wasn't here made the Bears worse. A great wide receiver can make an average quarterback good and a good quarterback great. That is nothing new. Everybody knows that. If you want to give Orton a real chance to help the Bears get back to the playoffs and then do something in the postseason, you have to give this team some help at the wide receiver position.

You have to go get a free agent, and you have to draft a wide receiver with your No. 1 pick. I'm not saying you do it like Matt Millen did with Detroit and draft a wide receiver with your No. 1 pick three years in a row, but you have to do it once. If you don't, you are not giving your team a chance to compete.

Let's get back to Orton. You can't blame this guy for the Bears not making the playoffs. He was throwing to Devin Hester, Marty Booker, and Brandon Lloyd, for crying out loud. Just remember who those guys are and realize that there's nothing close to an All-Pro in that bunch. Just how do you think Matt Cassel would have done throwing to those guys? He's up in New England taking over for Tom Brady in the first game of the season, and he did one hell of a job. There's no getting around that. But do you think he would have done that same job if he were here with the Bears and he was throwing to Brandon Lloyd or if Marty Booker was his main man? Devin Hester is a fast guy who can make plays, but is he an every-game, go-to receiver? I don't think so.

Now take a look at the other side of the coin. What if Orton is up in New England? Do you think he can find a way to get the ball to Randy Moss? Can he get the ball within reach of a wide-open Wes Welker? Of course he can, and you better believe it. The Patriots would not have done any worse if Orton was lining up at quarterback for them than they would have with Cassel. And I don't think the Bears would have done any better with Cassel than they did with Orton. I think they would have been worse. I don't think Cassel could have done as well with the Bears as Orton did.

So that's why I have a lot of questions about the way Angelo puts together the Bears. Oh, he does fine when it comes to putting together a defense, but when it comes to finding offensive talent, the man has a problem. I am so sick of the Bears being a team that tries to not make mistakes on offense and lets the defense and special teams do the job. Just once I would like to see the Bears as the team with the high-powered passing attack and capable of throwing for three touchdowns and 400 yards in a game. I want the Bears to have that kind of team.

I don't think it's ever going to happen under Angelo.

2

Cubs

Unlovable Losers

Let me tell you about the Cubs. I look at the back of the uniforms and I see their last names. They need to take off those names and replace them with two words—false hope.

That's what the fans have about the Cubs. The TV cameras show the fans in the stands hoping, clapping, praying that this is the year that good things will happen. They all have hope that the Cubs will turn things around and win a championship. It's nothing but false hope.

No matter what kind of team they have had, it's always been false hope. Whether they had a lot of stars or they had a bunch of over-achieving hustlers, they've only been a false hope kind of team. Take the 2008 season. This was a team with All-Stars up and down the lineup, and that's been the case a lot of times. They've had seven or eight All-Stars, and what have they won? Nothing. Oh, excuse me. They beat the Braves in the National League Division Series in 2003 prior to losing to the Marlins. That's all they have to show in 100 years. Yet they are all out there praying and hoping like a miracle is about to happen.

Actually, the more All-Stars they have, the more it scares me. When they have the guys who hustle, scratch, and claw, that's when I think they might have a chance. But last year was the top when it came to false hope. They were clearly the best team in the National League throughout the regular season, but in the end, what did that matter? They needed to show something when it was all on the line. I don't think you saw that.

 "No matter what kind of team they have had, it's always been false hope.

Let's go back to the 2003 playoffs and the Bartman thing. Steve Bartman was blamed for the Cubs losing those playoffs. What he did— reaching over for a foul ball—happened in one game and changed nothing of what was going on in that game. The outfielder was Moises Alou. He wasn't exactly a guy known for diving for balls or jumping for balls. Alou and defense did not go together, yet there he was, stomping his feet and jumping up and down when the kid got his hands on a ball that Alou wasn't going to catch anyway.

I have received plenty of calls from people who were sitting close to Bartman and tried for that ball. They still thank God that they weren't the ones who got their hands on it and got blamed for what happened. The guy next to Bartman went after the ball a lot more vigorously than Bartman did. That's clear when you look at it on videotape.

Then you have Dusty Baker, sitting in the dugout and doing nothing. He didn't quell the situation, and that's unconscionable. He could have gone out to the mound and talked to Mark Prior, slowed things down a little bit, and calmed everything down. Instead, he sat in the dugout with his arms folded and shook his head.

Did Steve Bartman boot the double play ground ball that was hit to shortstop? No. That was Alex Gonzalez. So why in the world does this kid trying to catch a foul ball get blamed? The whole thing—curses,

Cubs fans celebrate after the Cubs beat the Chicago White Sox 7–1 in an inter-league game on Sunday, June 22, 2008, at Wrigley Field. It's nothing but false hope. (AP Photo/Nam Y. Huh)

billy goats, whatever, it's all ridiculous. They're only making excuses for not making winning plays when the game was on the line.

That's the thing with this team. There's always someone or something to blame—but it's never the guys looking in the mirror. Why is that? Why are there always excuses and nobody ever stepping forward? It's the sun and all those hot day games—that's what we heard for years. "Oh, if only we had lights and played night games"—how has that one worked out? Excuses are just that, and they are always transparent. You can see right through them.

And these excuses and curses: the goat…have you ever heard anything more ridiculous than that one? The carnival atmosphere of the neighborhood? The partying going on in the bleachers? All excuses and all bulls--t.

Okay, so even if you want to blame Bartman for that play, go ahead. But what happened next? The world didn't stop spinning, and the game didn't come to an end. The Cubs still had plenty of opportunities. Even with Baker doing nothing but sitting on his hands, Prior got what should have been a double-play grounder that would have gotten him out of the inning, but Gonzalez—supposedly a great fielder—booted it.

Why don't they call it the Alex Gonzalez game? He was the one who had more to do with the Cubs losing than some kid in the stands. His name ought to be in the legacy and not a kid who just had some bad luck to be sitting where he was sitting and making the mistake of going after a foul ball.

The more time that goes by, the more unforgivable that game is as far as the Cubs are concerned. I don't think any other manager would have done nothing the way Baker did. Certainly not Lou Piniella—he would have always kept in mind that it's his responsibility as manager to win the game.

Piniella is certainly a better game manager than Baker was on his best day. He knows how to make a double switch, and I think that's something that Baker struggled with, even though he's always been a National League guy. Piniella is also more of a calming influence.

"Piniella is certainly a better game manager than Baker was on his best day."

That's saying something, because I remember Piniella when he was really fiery and would get involved and down and dirty with his team. He'll still do that every once in a while, but what I like about him is that he won't panic. If somebody gets hurt and can't play, Piniella doesn't roll his eyes and say, "Woe is me." Instead, he accepts it and moves on. That's what good leadership is all about.

Think about the opposite situation. If somebody gets injured or suspended and the manager starts talking about how unfair the situation is, he's giving his team a reason to give up or at least start thinking about excuses.

Look at the 2008 season. During the year, the Cubs lost guys like Alfonso Soriano, Carlos Zambrano, Kerry Wood, and Reed Johnson. Piniella never threw up his hands and cried. He just accepted it and put the next guy in the lineup without making any excuses or changing expectations.

That's because Piniella put together a baseball team and not just a bunch of individuals looking for stats or big numbers. They are on the right path. But even with the improvements they made and the leadership they had under Piniella, how could they really compete in the postseason when they knew that, no matter what happened, they would have to play an American League team?

The difference between the two leagues is absolutely staggering. The National League is weaker than it has been in 40, 50, or 60 years. The American League won 46 games more than they lost in interleague competition. How much more do you need to know than that when you're talking about the strength of the two leagues?

I had a bet with Mike Murphy, the midday personality of WSCR, on the interleague competition. We bet $10 per game and after the first week of competition, we changed it to $11 per game. By the time it was all said and done, he had to pay me $480.

The point is that the American League is much stronger than the National League, and it worked against the Cubs quite a bit. I think there were maybe four or five American League teams that were probably better than they were. And even if the Cubs were good enough to compete with those American League teams, the fact that they had to face poor National League teams on a daily basis hurt them when it came to getting ready for the postseason.

Cubs vs. Sox

Baseball can be a slow-moving game, and it lends itself to a lot of talking—and arguing. What is better than arguing baseball, especially Cubs and Sox?

You will argue to the death for your team. The buddies that I had growing up, you would play baseball or play softball and then when it got too dark you'd stop playing and start arguing. I grew up in Rogers Park, and we used to hang out at the corner of Thorndale and Glenwood and argue. Who's better—Bill Melton or Ron Santo? If you were a Cubs fan, you'd talk about Billy Williams. If you were a Sox fan, you would talk about Floyd Robinson. I can remember taking up the cause of Floyd Robinson and arguing with my Cubs buddies that he was actually better than Billy Williams. Was it ridiculous? Of course it was. Billy Williams had all the credentials in his favor. But Floyd Robinson was on the Sox and he was my guy, so I stuck up for him.

There's a funny thing about those arguments. You remember them. Take the argument about Melton and Santo. Over the long haul of their careers, Santo had better overall numbers than Melton. However, Melton did win the American League home-run crown, in 1971. In those years, he was better than Santo. The *coup de grace* came when the Cubs traded Santo to the Sox, and he and Melton were on the team at the same time. Which one did they move to second base? Santo. They told him, "Hey, go over to second base. We have our third baseman."

And let me tell you something about Santo. Everyone may love him now because he has been through so much and he's such a nice guy, but the word on the street back then was that he was not so nice. Santo was not the kind of guy who would go out of his way to help a young player. That's when Jorge Orta was coming up for the Sox, and Santo did not show him the ropes. Orta had to learn everything on his own because Santo was not going to help out.

After the Cubs traded Ron Santo to the White Sox, he was moved from third base to second. This photo was taken on Tuesday, July 3, 1974. (AP Photo/Fred Jewell)

 "Santo was not the kind of guy who would go out of his way to help a young player."

I think you take those allegiances with you as you get older. Some of the emotion goes out of it as the years go by, but we become passionate again during the big moments. I have buddies who are Cubs fans who I know were rooting for the Sox in 2005 when they were in the World Series. They would never admit it to anybody else, but when the Sox finally made it to the World Series, these people were rooting for the White Sox. They admitted it to me.

There's always been resentment between the Sox fans and the Cubs fans. That's just the way it has been for a long time. Cubs fans get everything they want, and they are the darlings. White Sox fans are just the other guys.

If a little kid gets hit with a foul ball at Wrigley Field, everyone is so concerned and it's a big story for two weeks. The same thing happens on the South Side at U.S. Cellular Field, and it's a one-day story. Go rub some dirt on it, you'll be fine. The kid is back at the ballpark the next day.

Things have been inequitable around the two teams for a very long time, and if you are with the White Sox, you are going to come to resent it. They put it in your face every day, how can you not?

All this happens even though the White Sox have the better stadium, the better facility, the better locker room, and the better parking. They couldn't be more kid-friendly with all the activities they make available to the little kids. The Cubs have a dump of a ballpark that was actually in disrepair. Pieces of Wrigley were falling down and hitting people. The place should have been condemned and knocked down. Instead, Major League Baseball put up netting in the stands, did some repairs, and now they can't wait to expand this facility.

Wrigley Field

It's an advantage to play at Wrigley Field. It kills the Cubs to play at Wrigley Field. You hear these points made every day. I think Cubs fans think on certain days that it's a help and that on other days it really hurts them. I'm not sure, either. The bottom line is that it may not matter at all. It's a ballpark, and it's a place to play. It doesn't hurt or help.

But one thing I do know is that there have been a lot of visiting ballplayers who liked to play at Wrigley Field. Mike Schmidt couldn't wait to get to Wrigley Field and start hitting there. Greg Luzinski couldn't wait to get to hit at Wrigley. What about Dave Kingman?

When he was wearing a Mets uniform, oh boy, did he love to hit at Wrigley Field. All these guys circled their Wrigley Field dates on their calendars. All they wanted to know was when they were going to play day ball and when they were going to face Cubs pitching. They wanted to go out and kick the Cubs' butts and wanted to raise their averages, home run totals, and RBI totals.

They loved the configuration of the ballpark, and they loved the day baseball. It should have been an advantage for the Cubs. But instead of just going out and playing, they were thinking about having to play in the sun and how hot it got. They looked at the schedule and would see that they had 81 home games—all in the day. And maybe 30 day games were on the road. So while other teams were playing 100 to 115 night games, the Cubs were playing 100 to 115 day games. It was hot, and they did get worn down. But it became an even bigger disadvantage for them because they were thinking about how much better it would be if they had night games themselves and if Wrigley Field had lights.

The other part of the situation is that the Cubs never used the familiarity with Wrigley Field to their advantage. When you play at a place every single day, you should know all the angles of the ballpark. You know how the sun is at a certain point of the year and how the shadows affect the fielders, the pitchers, and the hitters. That familiarity with the ballpark should have worked to their advantage and to their opponents' disadvantage, but it was just the opposite. Opponents, guys like Eddie Matthews of the Braves, Stan Musial of the Cardinals, and Willie Mays of the Giants went out and played at Wrigley and enjoyed it. They didn't complain about the sun, the heat, or the shadows. They wanted to get the game over with and win it so they could go enjoy themselves in Chicago. The Cubs? They wanted to feel sorry for themselves because they had it tough with the sun in their eyes.

The Cubs never had the right kind of players. Here's a mixed group from different years, but they had Dennis Eckersley, Bill Caudill, and

Willie Hernandez—guys who would go out and drink and get themselves in trouble. Eckersley's situation as an alcoholic is well-documented. Caudill liked to drink. I once saw Willie Hernandez out all night, and he was still shooting pool at 9:00 PM when he was half in the bag. Instead of going home and getting their rest, Cubs players were going out, enjoying the nightlife, and doing the town like it was a unique thing for them. They were in Chicago every time they played at home, but where was the self-discipline? Why didn't the players take care of themselves and their responsibilities to be prepared for the next day's game? I'm not saying it was every Cubs player, but it was enough of them over the years that the team could not get a proper home-field advantage.

"The Cubs never had the right kind of players."

And they really needed a home-field advantage back in those days because the other teams were so talented. When you are facing a Willie Mays, a Hank Aaron, a Roberto Clemente, and a Stan Musial, you need to get any edge you can and take advantage of it. The Cubs weren't forced to account for themselves by management, and the players did not police themselves.

Take it from a guy who used to work middays and drink pretty hard himself. If you like to drink and you're getting off in the afternoon when most of the people in your business don't get off until late at night, you are going to use that time to drink. You can do a lot of damage when you get off at 4:00 PM and go out. You need to have that discipline and take care of yourself and take care of your game. You can't be going out in the middle of the week and do it three or four times a week. If a player does that, he's dragging in the game.

You see a ball hit to the outfield and somebody reaches for it two or three times before he can pick it up, that's when you have issues.

To be a major leaguer at anything, you have to be at your best and do everything you can to make yourself be at your best. You can't be draining yourself by going out and drinking and doing all that stuff. You have to work at it. When the other team is looking after itself and doing everything it can and you're not, that's when you have some trouble.

It's not just baseball, either. I'm talking about any of the sports. Take the San Antonio Spurs. They are just about the straightest team you could imagine. On their team plane, they play Scrabble. They're not playing Tonk or cards or anything else like most of the other NBA teams do. They may get ridiculed for that, but that's who they are. They are not partying guys. Tim Duncan isn't going out at 1:00 or 2:00 AM. He's in bed, and he's asleep. Tony Parker isn't out at that hour either, and why would he want to be? (He is, after all, married to Eva Longoria.) He might have been going out before he met Eva, but I don't think it was ever a big issue. On that team, if you don't keep your mind on your business and do your job, you are gone after a year. They simply don't put up with crap or anything. You have to be able to do your job or else you don't stay around. They had Dennis Rodman—just two seasons. They had Vernon Maxwell, too. He was gone after a year.

The '69 Cubs

Those guys were partying maniacs. Look what happened. They got overtaken by the Mets. Sure, the Mets had a great team with all that quality pitching—Tom Seaver, Jerry Koosman, guys like that. But the Cubs had 61 wins by the All-Star break and could have put their foot on the Mets' throats and never did it. Shame on them. They had an opportunity to take care of business, and they never did.

The Cubs let the Mets hang around…hang around…and hang around until the Mets were finally back in it, and by then it was too late. Instead of taking care of their own business, the Cubs started watching the scoreboard, hoping and praying the Mets would lose. It didn't have to be that way. The Cubs took their foot off the accelerator and gave the Mets new life.

A lot of that was on Leo Durocher. He was one of those managers who didn't believe in playing his bench. The '69 Cubs are one of those teams that are the best examples of why you do play your bench and rest your regulars. Everybody needs a break. Especially when you are playing in the heat. Especially when your guys are starting to press. Durocher didn't like his bench, and he didn't play it.

They don't do that anymore. When the White Sox won in 2005, Ozzie Guillen used his bench. Look at Mike Scioscia of the Angels. He may be the best manager in the game, and he rests his guys and uses his bench better than anyone else. He knows his players. He doesn't just sit them, either. He knows when one guy needs a rest and somebody else is fresh and needs to be in there.

Durocher was completely old school. Santo, you're my starting third baseman. Don Kessinger, you're my starting shortstop. Glenn Beckert, you're my second baseman. Ernie Banks, you know what, we're going to have our battles. You're a little bit too nice for me. I need a little more attitude. But you're still my starting first baseman. Randy Hundley, you're going to catch and you'll probably be behind the plate for about 150 games. I don't care if you get down to 120 pounds, you're still the catcher.

That was Leo's take on it, and he ran that team into the ground. The same thing happened not even 10 years later when the Red Sox buried the Yankees in July and then New York started to come back and the Red Sox started to die. Nevertheless, Don Zimmer basically trotted out the same starting lineup every single game. He didn't play his bench, either, and the Yankees caught them and eventually won the division in that famous one-game playoff.

Those two teams both blew it. Durocher didn't play his bench in 1969, and Zimmer didn't play his in '78. I think managers took note of how both of those teams blew it, and you don't see managers ignore their bench very much anymore. Teams don't run out of gas as much. Teams still blow the leads and choke but not out of exhaustion the way the 1969 Cubs and '78 Red Sox did.

Another thing about Durocher—he didn't care who he or his players offended. Santo clicking his heels is one of the iconic images of that '69 team. Now that was really rubbing it in the faces of the Cubs' opponents. Did Durocher warn Santo about that and tell him not to do that anymore? No. He encouraged him to do it, and it just made people even madder.

When you're a competitor and you see the guy in the other dugout rubbing it in, that just makes you madder. That's how Santo left the field. Jumping up and down and clicking his heels. A team that might not have cared so much the next time they played the Cubs was now fired up for a huge game.

Think about it. The minute you see that guy jump up and click his heels, you're mad. But then when you're having dinner or having a cocktail at the hotel bar, you're absolutely seething. If I'm one of those players, I'm saying, "I'm going to beat that son of a bitch the next day. I don't want to see that guy do it again."

I have to say that I think that whole heel-clicking thing has done more to keep Santo out of the Hall of Fame than anything. Especially now when it's the veterans committee doing the voting. When they get behind closed doors, they are remembering things like that, and they use it when they vote to keep him out of the Hall of Fame.

And if they do hold it against him, it's absolutely deserved. I have never seen another player do anything like that since. He ran down the left-field line—with his back to the other team—jumping up and clicking his heels. And once again, the ballpark is the culprit. The clubhouse was way down in left field. If the clubhouse was behind the dugout, nobody would have ever known because they wouldn't have seen him jumping up and down.

> "I think that whole heel-clicking thing has done more to keep Santo out of the Hall of Fame than anything."

But because that clubhouse was way down the left-field line, he could work up some speed, jump up there pretty good, and click those heels. Basically he was ridiculing the other team. No matter how it's spun today, he was rubbing it in their faces back then.

And believe me, the word got around. There may not have been cell phones or the Internet back then, but there sure were telephones. You don't think a Brave called a Cardinal or a Phillie called a Dodger and talked about it? "You better watch out for that Santo. When they win, he clicks his heels."

Santo put himself in the position he's in today with the Hall of Fame, and he did it with Durocher's encouragement. The Cubs thought they couldn't be beaten. When they started to lose and other teams caught up with them, it all came back and bit them in the ass when the season was on the line. The Cubs paid a big price, and Santo is still paying for it.

Ryne Sandberg

One guy who has really surprised me over the years in Ryne Sandberg. When he was in his heyday for the Cubs—and what a great ballplayer he was—he didn't say a word. He was as quiet as he could be, and you got the feeling that he really didn't have anything to say. He would just go about his business, make his plays in the field, hit a home run

Known in his playing days for his quiet demeanor, Cubs Hall of Famer Ryne Sandberg let his bat and his Gold Glove speak for him. (AP Photo)

or get a big hit, and then go home and get ready for the next game. It didn't appear he had much else on his mind.

But as the years have gone by, it seems that the quiet Sandberg who wouldn't even say "boo" when he was a player is really a much different guy than we all thought. I mean, I would have been surprised to see him become a minor league manager, but I think he is doing it the right way and now I would be surprised if he didn't become the Cubs' manager. I think they are grooming him for the job, and he will most likely take over when Lou Piniella decides to retire. That's how far Sandberg has come.

I think he's got something there. I think he has a lot more fire than anybody thought he had as a player. I'm not knocking him, because he did play hard when he was a star with the Cubs, but you just couldn't see what was going on inside him or what was motivating him. It seemed like he was just one of those guys who went out there and played. He played well and he helped his team win a lot of games, but did it look like it really mattered to him?

> **"I think he has a lot more fire than anybody thought he had as a player."**

Certainly not on the outside. He didn't show his emotions, and I think that bothered some people as the years went by. But as a minor league manager, he has stood up for his players on a regular basis, and he has made the point that he will fight for his team whenever they need him to. I think that's something all good managers have to do. They have to let their players know that their manager will be there for them if things get tough and the calls start to go against them. You can't just be willing to sit there and take it. Sandberg has thrown his support behind his players, and they know it. The Cubs management also knows it, and that's why they keep promoting him. Piniella is not going to be around forever, and if Sandberg continues to grow on the job, I think he will get the opportunity someday to manage the team that he did such an outstanding job playing for.

He is throwing himself into managing the way he threw himself into playing. He could do it all, and I think most people will agree that when the Cubs won that National League East title in 1984, Sandberg was a big part of that team. I guess you can make a pretty good argument for Rick Sutcliffe because he was so effective (16–1) after he came to the Cubs from Cleveland, but I still have to go with Sandberg because he was there from Game 1.

He really made it big the day he hit two home runs off of the Cardinals' Bruce Sutter to tie the game up twice in the late innings. Sutter was the best relief pitcher in the game at the time, and it was obvious at that moment that Sandberg had arrived. I think that was the instant you knew the Cubs would be in the race for the pennant all the way until the end, and that was the moment that Sandberg became a big part of what was important in Chicago sports.

He had a great and long playing career with the Cubs, and I think he is doing all the right things to make sure he is ready whenever he gets his chance to manage them. Some former players think it's their right to just move up to the big leagues and manage a team because of who they are, but Sandberg is doing all the hard work for very little money in order to get there. He's out of the spotlight, but he is really preparing.

You have to respect a guy like that. He is not asking for superstar treatment, and I don't think he ever has. All he wants to do is improve at managing and get his players prepared for their big-league careers. He is not looking for the limelight or trying to get back in the headlines. He's a guy who seems to have both feet on the ground and is doing everything he needs in order to get where he wants. Whenever that opportunity comes, I think he will know what he's doing.

You have to respect Sandberg and all the work he is doing. I know I do.

Dusty Baker

Dusty Baker never gave the Cubs what they needed.

Forget about getting their money's worth, because that wasn't the issue. This is a team that sells out Wrigley Field every game. Selling tickets is a done deal for the Cubs.

But when the Cubs hired Dusty Baker, he was supposed to be a winner who would take them to the next level. He did not live up to the hype. I didn't see the kind of leadership ability from Baker that

Dusty Baker took a backseat approach to leadership that failed to make the Cubs winners in the postseason. (AP Photo/James A. Finley)

the Cubs wanted or needed. He was more than content to sit on the bench, working his toothpick and wearing that Cubs jacket. I think he was happiest when he didn't even have to move. He looked like he was posing for a statue.

When they needed leadership from him he sat there and went along for the ride. When things got tough for the Cubs, Baker sat and watched.

People may say that a manager is only going to do certain things, like make a lineup and do the double-switches in the National League. Let me state for the record that Baker did not do a very good job when he had double-switches to make. The lineup choices? He had to get permission from Sammy Sosa, didn't he? After all, he didn't move Sosa in the batting lineup until the two had had an "amicable conversation." Why does a manager have to get permission from a player to move him in the lineup? It doesn't make any sense. You do that and you're giving away all the authority you had as a manager.

Maybe you felt like you didn't have any in the first place, so maybe that was the case with Baker. Maybe he didn't have the confidence in himself or maybe he was just a little too comfortable. But any way you look at it, he just didn't look like he was in charge for the Cubs.

 **"I didn't see the kind of leadership ability from Baker that the Cubs wanted or needed."**

That was never more the case than in Game 6 of the 2003 playoffs against the Marlins. The whole world knows the circumstances with Steve Bartman and the foul ball, but there was obviously a lot more to it than that.

Even before the sixth game, there were plenty of signs that Dusty Baker was not going to keep his team on edge and that he wasn't going to get the most out of them. As a manager, that's just about the same as abandoning your post. Once a playoff series is over, there's plenty of time to look back at what went right and what went wrong. There's no reason to look back as a series is in progress and tell everyone how good you are and what you're doing right. That tells your own team that you're satisfied with what's been going on, and it lights a fire under your opponent.

That is exactly what happened after the second game in the series. You wouldn't think that was such a big deal because the Cubs had just tied the Marlins at 1–1 and went on to win Games 3 and 4 and take a seemingly insurmountable 3–1 lead. But that's exactly what happened when the Cubs won the second game at Wrigley Field to tie the series at 1–1.

The Cubs won the game 12–3, and they had hammered the Florida pitching staff. Alex Gonzalez, of all people, hit two home runs to lead the way. The Cubs had big hits throughout the game and had thoroughly dominated the Marlins.

But it was only the second game of the series and the Cubs had just tied up the NLCS—not won the seventh game. So how did Baker react to the win? He started comparing Gonzalez—Gonzalez!—to past World Series heroes. That's great. You take a guy who was as streaky as they get and was not going to scare anybody and say he could be a World Series hero like Gene Tenace because he hit two home runs. That was ridiculous.

Baker also portrayed his team as unstoppable just because they had scored 12 runs. "When you have the kind of offense we have, sooner or later you are going to get it together," Baker said. "I'm not surprised."

That last little throwaway sentence—"I'm not surprised"—is not exactly the best way to keep your team hungry. You still have to win three games, and you make it seem like it's just a matter of course that you're going to score runs like that whenever you want just because you show up. It's one thing to point out your team's strengths, but it's quite another to assume your team is so good that it can score at will against a top-level opponent when you're playing for the National League title and when you're the Chicago Cubs—you just don't make a statement like that. It comes off as smug.

That doesn't do your own team any good, and it really gets under the skin of your opponent. Jack McKeon was managing the Marlins in that series, and he was the perfect guy to settle down his team and get them heading in the right direction.

McKeon had been with the Padres in 1984 when they came back to beat the Cubs after losing the first two games, including the first game by a 13–0 margin. He heard the Cubs and their manager crowing after Game 2. The Game 3 matchup had Kerry Wood going up against left-handed pitcher Mark Redman, and both pitchers had won 14 games during the season. The game was in Miami, and McKeon was damn angry that everyone conceded the game to the Cubs.

"Now let me get this straight," McKeon said sarcastically. "The game is in our park, and the series is tied. Our pitcher won 14 games and their pitcher won 14 games, but we don't have a chance. It's all about them. That's my understanding. We don't have a chance."

It turned out the experts were right as the Cubs won Game 3 (and Game 4 for that matter), but the tone of the Cubs' remarks in general and Dusty Baker in particular stuck with the Marlins' manager and his players. It played at least a small role in their ability to stay alive and keep fighting against the Cubs.

Remember how casual Baker was when the Cubs lost Game 5? The team got handled easily by Josh Beckett, who pitched a great game to get the Marlins back in the series. It didn't seem to both Baker at all. He thought because the Cubs were coming home for Games 6 and 7 that it was all over. The combination of Mark Prior and Kerry Wood was supposed to be unbeatable, and while Game 5 was going on, Baker was thinking about the Red Sox and Yankees and which team he would rather play in the World Series.

He wasn't on the bench in Game 5, fighting and scrapping to get his team back in the game, he conceded it because he was happy to be going back home. That doesn't work in the playoffs. You can't give up on any game and assume you will get it done when you return home. That was another big mistake.

Not only is it a mistake for that game, it's a mistake because of the message that it sends to your team. The message you send is that it's no big deal to lose one game because your talent and firepower are so superior that you are going to win when you get back home to close out the series. When you manage like that and you give that kind of attitude, you're hurting your players instead of preparing them to be their best. It's a fat-cat attitude when you just think you are flat-out better than your opponent.

"When you manage like that and you give that kind of attitude, you're hurting your players instead of preparing them to be their best."

And then there was Game 6. There was Dusty sitting in the dugout with his toothpick and Cubs jacket, rocking back and forth and taking it all in. He was probably considering whether he would have his son on his lap when taking questions from the reporters after the game or whether he would handle that one by himself.

So the Cubs had a nice 3–0 lead in the eighth inning when Luis Castillo came up with a man on and one out and he hit a foul ball toward the stands. Steve Bartman went after the foul ball, and Moises Alou didn't catch it. Alou stomped his feet and threw a fit when he didn't catch the ball.

At the same time, Baker is just sitting in the dugout and he isn't moving. He's taking it in like he has a ticket for the game. He doesn't go out to calm down Prior or say anything to Alou. Instead, he's just watching as Prior is clearly starting to sweat. Prior ends up walking Castillo, and Baker does nothing. He gives up a single to Ivan Rodriguez, and Baker does nothing. Miguel Cabrera hits what should be a double-play ground ball to Gonzalez who boots the ball, and all hands are safe.

Baker goes out to talk to Prior, but he doesn't take him out. Prior is clearly shaken and has lost his confidence, but Baker doesn't see it and he leaves him in. Then Derrek Lee hit a double and the tying runs are in.

Then Baker brings in Kyle Farnsworth to get through the rest of the inning. He has Farnsworth throw an intentional walk, and then the Marlins get the lead run on a sacrifice fly. Another intentional walk loads the bases again and Farnsworth, one of the least reliable pitchers I've ever seen, gives up a bases-loaded double. Another hit made it 8–3 Marlins, and the devastation was complete.

Baker did almost nothing and when he finally made a move, it was to Farnsworth. Unbelievable. Cubs fans had that look of doom on their faces, and you just knew that it was over. When you're a manager who is content with his spot in the world and just wants to feel good about his team and his job, you're not giving the team the right message. You are supposed to create urgency. Dusty Baker's team followed his lead. They were satisfied and happy and ultimately came up short. That's no way to live your life, and it is certainly no way to manage.

2008: A Wasted Opportunity

The Cubs are everybody's darlings. Is there any doubt? That's the way it's been since Harry Caray went to the North Side and started broadcasting with the Cubs. That was the start of the Cubs growth in popularity, and it has continued long after his death.

Even as the pressure has grown as the World Series drought continues, you can't argue with the team's popularity. It really looked like 2008 would give the Cubs a legitimate chance to win the National League pennant and finally get to the World Series for the first time since 1945.

This was the best team in the National League during the regular season by a good amount. I'm not saying that teams like the Phillies and the Dodgers couldn't compete with them, but there is no doubt that the Cubs were the better regular-season team. But when the playoffs started against the Dodgers, the Cubs had absolutely nothing and got swept in the first round for the second straight year.

There were reasons for it. I'm not saying you could see it coming, but one of the reasons that the Cubs were vulnerable is that they played in such a weak division. I mean, the National League just doesn't compare with the American League, but the Central was just awful and that's why the Cubs were able to run away from the rest of the division. I know Milwaukee made the playoffs, but they had plenty of flaws that were obvious when they played the Cubs.

On the other hand, Charlie Manuel and the Phillies at least had to fight the Mets to win the division title—so they were challenged. The Dodgers had to come from behind to catch Arizona. Both of those teams had to fight through it. Unlike the Cubs, they couldn't just run and hide. That made both of those teams tougher to beat in the playoffs.

I know Lou Piniella said that his team just got cold at the wrong time, like it was just a coincidence and that it could have happened to any team and that the bad luck just happened to bite the Cubs at the wrong time. I don't know if he really believes that because I don't believe it.

There was just nothing there. The Cubs had a two-run lead in the fifth inning of the first game, and Ryan Dempster was on the mound. After a season in which he pitched consistently, he had no control and he loaded the bases, giving free passes left and right. He gave up a grand slam to James Loney, and the Dodgers had the lead.

Okay, that's not good, but it was only the fifth inning of the first game of the series. But instead of responding in the bottom of the fifth or the bottom of the sixth, the Cubs were just stunned and couldn't get up off the mat. I hate to say it, but it was like the 2003 National League Championship Series between the Cubs and the Marlins. Everything was going their way until the Steve Bartman incident when the team fell apart and did not respond. (Not that it was Bartman's fault.) When things went wrong in 2003, the Cubs didn't answer and it was like watching an accident. You couldn't take your eyes off of it.

Well, that's how it was against the Dodgers. No response at all when the Dodgers fired their shot. It was a complete collapse, and it was completely unacceptable. It was all bad—the hitting, the pitching, the base running, and the fielding. I don't think I ever saw anything worse than those errors in the second game when all four members of the infield made errors. But you could also say the clutch hitting was just as bad because they couldn't get a hit in the clutch.

 "I don't think I ever saw anything worse than those errors in the second game when all four members of the infield made errors."

This was a team that had gotten clutch hits and came from behind all season long. Why was it so dead in Wrigley Field after Loney's grand slam? Why couldn't they come back at all? It seemed like it was the pressure of being in the playoffs and trying to win a series and then win the pennant and get to the World Series and win that was just way too much for them. If that's the case, how will they ever get over those hurdles in the future? You are always going to have that pressure every time you get to the playoffs. It's just a matter of going out and playing and not thinking about anything else other than the pitch you are about to see, the ground ball you are about to make, or the pitch that you have to make next. Whatever happened 10, 20, or 40 years ago doesn't matter. It's obvious that the history bothers the team even if they don't admit it. It's obvious from their play.

That pressure has been around every time the Cubs have made the playoffs or even gotten close. In 1969 when they had the big lead against the Mets, that's probably when it started. But in 1984, the expectations were high against the Padres in the playoffs, and they've been there every time.

But they were never higher than they were this year. I'm thinking a lot about Be-Be when I say that. Because she's been a Cubs fan forever and I mean a real Cubs fan. She's always been able to keep her expectations in check and was always pretty realistic. But not in 2008. Like a lot of Cubs fans, she thought that the 100-year thing meant something and that they were going to be able to turn things around because of it.

Lou Piniella had no answers at all. The only thing he could do is point out the obvious and show that he was just as frustrated as any fan. I don't think that's what you want from your manager.

"Let me tell you this: You can play postseason baseball for now to another hundred years, but if you score six runs in three games, it's going to be another hundred years before we win," manager Lou Piniella said. "We just didn't hit. We had opportunities, and you have to take advantage of them. This is six games I've managed now in the postseason, and we have scored just 12 runs. That doesn't get it done. I just don't see it in the postseason."

We know that too, Lou. It's not just a matter of knowing the score and knowing how things got done. It's like the Cubs were overwhelmed with the weight of 100 years of not winning and played with that thing on their backs. Of course, Piniella wants to change that, and I think he's trying, but it's up to the players—and they weren't up to it against the Dodgers in 2008 or the Diamondbacks in 2007.

Piniella has to take some accountability for the playoff loss because he got outmanaged by Joe Torre, who put the right players on the field and got the right results. When you're Piniella and you're throwing Kosuke Fukudome out there in the starting lineup for the first two games, that's hurting your team. I mean, here was a guy who was obviously afraid of the ball, and that meant he had no business being in the lineup. I don't understand why he would play Fukudome when it was obvious he was more interested in not getting hurt than he was in standing in the batter's box and battling. He was always in a hurry to get his butt out of there—especially when going up against a left-handed pitcher.

And then after the team collapsed against the Dodgers, Alfonso Soriano told the team's fans to be patient. Can you believe that? After 100 years, the fans are supposed to be patient? That's either the height of arrogance or the height of ignorance. Either way—and it's probably both—it couldn't be a more ridiculous thing to say.

"When you're Piniella and you're throwing Kosuke Fukudome out there in the starting lineup for the first two games, that's hurting your team."

"Keep patient because we have a very good team," Soriano said. "I think everybody is very disappointed. We have a very good team this year, but we didn't get it done. I hope next year we have a very good team then and go a little bit farther."

Soriano needs to look at himself in the mirror after his performance. How many hits did he get? How many clutch hits did he get? How many runs did he drive in? Where was he when the team was collapsing? He had one hit in 14 at bats. One hit! He struck out four times. No extra base hits. No runs batted in. He's saying to be patient? Give me a break. The stuff that he was saying after the game was just ridiculous.

"The best team is not always going to win in the postseason," Soriano said. "We had the best team in the league, but we didn't do nothing to win. Give them credit, but we didn't do anything. Yes, it's very sad because we didn't play better in the postseason. We have a better team than last year, but we didn't play good like a team. We have a very good team, but we have to get it down in the postseason. We expect a lot more than what we do on the field. I think everybody has to think about how we have to play in the playoffs because we've not played good enough to win. It's very disappointing because we want to go to the World Series, but we didn't put it together."

Didn't put it together? They didn't even win one game in the first round of the playoffs, for crying out loud, and Soriano ends it with a strikeout. Typical. I don't expect Soriano to have the same kind of knowledge about the Cubs history as their devoted fans. But any Cubs player who has been with the team say, about an hour and a half, starts to understand that it's been a 100 years since they won. So the last thing a guy should say at any point when talking about Cubs fans is that they need to be more patient. He's got a little bit of an excuse because of his background, but overall, you have to say it's really stupid.

But as bad as Soriano played in the series, you can't forget about Aramis Ramirez, either. Look at what he's done in the postseason in 2007 and 2008. The guy basically disappeared when the team needed him. I think it's ridiculous that the guy who wins the Hank Aaron Award (best hitter in the league) goes completely belly-up in the playoffs. Remember when he was hot and winning games with late-inning home runs? He did that during the regular season. But somehow when the playoffs come along, he couldn't produce.

Okay, so the Cubs lost and basically choked two years in a row. It's reached epic proportions with 100 years of still waiting for another World Series. Maybe they'll finally be able to get past it in the future because expectations will never be higher than they were in 2008. Not that the pressure won't be there, but expectations were so high because they had such a "great" team. Maybe fans will keep their expectations in check. Not their hopes, which will always be high, but their expectations. If that's the case, it just might make it a little easier on the players in the future.

The Grace Factor

I loved Mark Grace as a player for the Cubs. I give him a lot of credit because he was always playing for a new contract and that meant he was always giving it his all on the field. He did not have a long guaranteed contract like a lot of players who rest on their laurels and try to live off their past headlines.

Mark Grace always gave it his all on the field— even when the Cubs lost. (AP Photo/Beth A. Keiser)

He's trying to be a "tell it like it is" kind of broadcaster, and he really opened fire on the Cubs after they lost in the playoffs. I'm not going to argue with him and say he was wrong. However, is he really the guy who should be criticizing the team? I mean, he was a Cub himself, and what did he ever win? He may have done pretty well with the bat and tried to be the Cubs' answer to Will Clark when they played the Giants in the 1989 playoffs, but the Cubs did not win the series. They did not beat the Giants in the playoffs, and they did not go to the World Series. So what did Mark Grace ever win, and why is he the guy who's leading the critics?

"They screwed it up, honestly," Grace said after the Cubs lost. "That's twice now that this same group of players has gone out and played tight.... I mean, come on, dude, are you kidding me? They got swept by the Diamondbacks, and they got swept by the Dodgers. Just went out and played tight. Honestly, I was very disappointed in what I saw, especially this year.

"So what did Mark Grace ever win, and why is he the guy who's leading the critics?"

"They were, in my opinion, by far the best team in the National League," said Grace. "And to get swept out, they really should be humiliated. It shouldn't have been over when Loney hit that grand slam, because you're only down two runs with five innings to play and that team just laid down. The place turned into a tomb. Damn, you're just down two, and you had come back all year. The team laid down.

"I wanted only good things for them, and I was disappointed."

You can't argue with anything that Grace said. But is he really the guy you want to be criticizing the team? I'm not saying he doesn't have the right, because everybody has the right. I criticize teams, players, and coaches all the time—when they deserve it. But there's something about it when it comes from your own family that isn't right.

3

White Sox

Ozzie Guillen

He's gotten into quite a bit of trouble with his mouth. So I guess Ozzie Guillen and I have a lot in common.

It may sound like a joke, but it's not. Ozzie is obviously a shoot-from-the-hip kind of guy who will say anything that's on his mind, and he doesn't care what anybody else thinks. I think you know that I'm going to say what I think and let the consequences be damned. If I was going to measure everything that came out of my mouth and worry about it, then I wouldn't be the guy who was on the Score from 1992 until 2008. I would have been back selling hot dogs a long time ago.

Guillen is not just a guy who will say what is on his mind. I think he tries to light a fire under his players with the things he says, and that's fine.

But Ozzie wouldn't be this over-the-top motivator and manager if it wasn't for Jerry Reinsdorf. There are a lot of owners who wouldn't have known what to make of a guy who is as opinionated as Ozzie. They might bring him in for a talk and try to quiet him down once or maybe even twice, but after that, the guy would be sent packing. Most owners don't want a manager who is going to rock the boat or do anything too unconventional.

Ozzie Guillen looks at the crowd during the first inning of a baseball game against the Tampa Bay Rays in St. Petersburg, Florida, on April 20, 2008. (AP Photo/Joe Ranze)

"Ozzie wouldn't be this over-the-top motivator and manager if it wasn't for Jerry Reinsdorf."

That's what makes Jerry Reinsdorf such a great guy to work for. He could care less about the things that Ozzie says, and he only cares about the production of the team on the field. He wants to see a team that wins and competes on the field. He knows that Ozzie Guillen is going to say whatever pops into his brain without a lot of thought. He can say one thing at a given moment and then say something completely opposite five minutes later.

So he's not going to get in trouble with his owner for the things he says. When he goes too far the rest of the media gets involved. Like the time he used a gay slur to describe Jay Mariotti. He crossed a line there, but he was upset by Mariotti. I can understand that. Mariotti's a hit-and-run kind of guy, so it's frustrating. But the rules are pretty clear. You can't go after somebody based on race, ethnic background, or sexual preference. When he says something he shouldn't, he's got an employer who understands him and is not going to worry about it. But when you use a word like he did with Mariotti, it takes on a whole new meaning and gets a lot more than just the owner involved. That's what he has to be careful about.

As a strategist, he is very inconsistent. I don't always like his decisions, be it with his lineup or his pitching moves. I've criticized him on the air for some of his moves. He hears what is said about him, and he gets upset.

I don't know why. If you've won a World Series and you've been criticized on the radio or in print, you shouldn't care at all. If you're doing the best you can and you can look yourself in the mirror, you shouldn't care what anyone else thinks. But that's not Ozzie. He's got a red ass, and he lets criticism bother him. He's way too sensitive.

The real story is what Ozzie did as manager in 2005—he won a championship with the White Sox. Did any White Sox fan think it was possible? Well, of course we knew it was possible. But did we really think it would happen? It wasn't 100 years like the Cubs, but it was an awfully long time. He was the right manager for that playoff season.

I think the team was pretty loose by the time the playoffs started. They had a 15-game lead in early August, and they barely held on. Everyone tried to say, "there's no reason to panic," as the lead kept dwindling away. But there was reason to panic. No team had ever blown such a big lead. Not the 1951 Brooklyn Dodgers, not the 1969 Cubs, and not the 1978 Red Sox. This would have been the worst, but they managed to hang on, and it was a huge sigh of relief to have survived and not completed the biggest choke job ever. Cleveland may have played something like .700 ball while they were catching up, but the White Sox were losing games they should have won.

Nobody wants to call it choking, but that's just what the Sox were doing. Thank God they were able to pull out of it at the end and hold on to the lead and get into the postseason. They couldn't wait for the regular season to end and start the playoffs, and it almost cost them. But somehow, going through that process must have helped them, because they made an amazing run in the playoffs.

The 2005 World Series Champions

I have to say that I really didn't feel confident about the White Sox's chances when the playoffs started. They were playing the Red Sox, who had just ended their long World Series drought the year before. They were the defending champions, and they had learned how to win. Who thought they were going to have a problem with the White Sox after having to deal with the Yankees every year? But it was the White Sox who came out firing and playing with a ton of confidence.

You have to give Ozzie credit for that. He's a guy who is going to have his players ready and prepared. That's just what they were when they came out against the Red Sox. They were really sharp—not that it really mattered. The first game was all about home runs and bombing the ball all over the park. It ended up 14–2, and I think there was real confidence in the team after that. They played a very tough game in Game 2 and didn't lose a bit of that confidence even though Boston built a 4–0 lead. The Sox came back and took a 5–4 lead in the bottom of the fifth, and Mark Buehrle settled down after that and didn't give the Red Sox a thing. Bobby Jenks closed it out. It was a great job by Ozzie because he left Buehrle in when he struggled early and Jenks got two innings in.

When the Sox got to Boston, it was not supposed to be a sweep. This was the team that had rallied from 0–3 against the Yankees, so clearly they were not afraid. They appeared to be ready to make their move in the sixth because Manny Ramirez had homered and

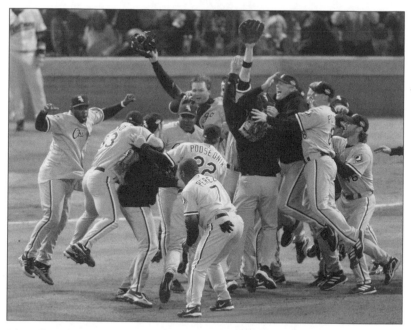

The White Sox storm to the mound after sweeping the Houston Astros to win the 2005 World Series on Wednesday, October 26, 2005, in Houston. (AP Photo)

Damaso Marte loaded the bases and Ozzie had to bring in Orlando "El Duque" Hernandez.

El Duque had clearly been a great big-game pitcher when he was with the Yankees, but how much did he have left? It looked like he would get slaughtered, but he was ready and got two pop-ups and a strikeout. The White Sox closed them out as Hernandez gave them two more innings, and Jenks finished the job again.

Unbelievable as it seemed, the White Sox were playing for the pennant. The Angels stood in their way and looked like they might crush the dreams of every White Sox fan who had been waiting since 1959 to see the team get back to the World Series. The Sox lost Game 1 by a 3–2 score—they just couldn't execute the small-ball kind of offense that had been one of their signatures that season. But Guillen knew his team had just lost one game and was far from defeated. Instead of criticizing anyone in the press, he went out of his way to praise starting pitcher Jose Contreras. "We didn't play well, and we didn't execute the way we can," Guillen said. "They played better than we did, but we will come back and play hard. Jose pitched great. They only had one legitimate hit all game."

By staying positive and praising his team in defeat, Guillen made it easy for his team to play much better in Game 2. That, of course, was the A.J. Pierzynski game. With two out in the bottom of the ninth with the score tied at 1–1, Pierzynski struck out swinging on a low fastball from the legendary Kelvim Escobar. As Angels and former Sox catcher Josh Paul rolled the ball back to the mound, Pierzynski took one step towards the Sox dugout and then ran to first. First-base umpire Doug Eddings called him safe, indicating that although Pierzynski had swung and missed, the ball had touched the ground.

As the Angels argued, they seemed to lose their focus, and worried about how such a call could go against them. Pinch runner Pablo Ozuna stole second, Joe Crede slammed the ball off the wall, and the Sox had tied the series.

But that win did more than tie up the series, it changed the whole feel. The Angels had played well but felt they had been robbed. They started feeling sorry for themselves, and after that they played as if they were worried about the next call or break that would go against them. But the White Sox enjoyed the most amazing pitching anyone had seen in decades during the postseason.

The Sox went to Anaheim and got three complete games from Jon Garland, Freddie Garcia, and Contreras, and won all three. It was simply amazing that they put together that kind of pitching. Paul Konerko had hit home runs in the first inning in Games 3 and 4, and as the Angels played tighter, the White Sox grew looser. It was amazing to see this team that had nearly blown the division in one of the most incredible choke jobs of all time come back and beat the

Red Sox in the first round of the playoffs and then win the pennant by beating the Angels.

"The White Sox enjoyed the most amazing pitching anyone had seen in decades during the postseason."

I felt like it was going to happen at that point. Ozzie was doing a great job, the pitching was on fire, and the White Sox were getting clutch hits and making things happen. Confidence was at an all-time high. I wasn't worried about the choke factor in the World Series. Not at all.

The Sox were playing the Astros, and they were playing the National League. This was not the National League of Pete Rose, Willie Mays, Bob Gibson, Hank Aaron, and Tom Seaver. The National League was just a shell of what it had been, and everybody knew it. The Astros simply didn't have the all-around talent to compete with the American League champions. If it was the Angels who had won the playoffs or if it had been the Red Sox, I would have said the same thing. But it was the White Sox, and they had it all out there in front of them.

Nothing against the Astros. Phil Garner had a fighting, hustling kind of team. They could play, they could execute, and they still had Craig Biggio and Lance Berkman, but there simply wasn't enough there to beat the White Sox. I knew it, and I knew Ozzie was not going to let the opportunity slip through his fingers.

There was no reason to be afraid of facing Roger Clemens in Game 1. He had a good season in the National League, but he was not seeing the same caliber of hitters that he had when he was in the American League. He was gone by the third inning, and the White Sox got the 5–3 win. The old-timers pointed out that the 1959 White Sox had also won the opener, bombing the Dodgers by an 11–0 score, but they lost the World Series in six games.

If there were any doubts in the hearts of some White Sox fans, they ended in the ninth inning of the second game. The Sox had been trailing 4–2 in the seventh and had come back to take the lead when Konerko hit a grand slam. The funny thing about it was there was no tension. Even though they had been trailing by two runs, there was no reason to think they were not going to come back. Konerko got the script and followed through.

But it was the bottom of the ninth after Houston came back to tie the game in the top of the inning that allowed everyone to know how the World Series would turn out. Scott Podsednik, all 125 pounds of him, came up to the plate with Brad Lidge on the mound. Lidge would go on to become a World Series and postseason hero with the Phillies three years later, but he was shaky in the postseason in 2005. He gave up a huge home run to Albert Pujols of St. Louis when it appeared the Astros were going to clinch the National League pennant against the Cardinals, and Lidge was still a little insecure.

Nobody knew that Lidge was so shaky that he would give up a game-winning homer to Podsednik, but that's just what he did. It was a low line drive that cut through the damp weather and drizzle and ended up in the stands.

That was it. The rest of the series may have been in Houston, but it didn't matter. They were close games, and it took 14 innings for Geoff Blum to give the White Sox a two-run homer and the win, but it was going to happen. Garner wasn't happy with his team and said that his team's performance was embarrassing, but it really wasn't. They were beaten by a better team.

A small-ball run in the eighth and a great performance by both Garcia and the bullpen gave the White Sox a 1–0 win. The final out was the moment that every White Sox fan had been waiting for all their lives. Orlando Palmeiro hit a slow roller to short. It would have been easy for Juan Uribe to screw it up or find a way not make the play, but he picked up the ball on a dead run and fired a strike to give the White Sox the title.

Once they got to the World Series, I really expected it—not necessarily a sweep but at least a convincing win. The team had been through their hard times during the regular season, but Ozzie had given this team the focus and the kick in the pants it needed. It was the culmination of every White Sox fan's dream, and it felt even better than you imagined it would. It was the greatest moment possible for any White Sox fan, and Guillen had given Reinsdorf and Kenny Williams the managing job they had wanted when they hired him the year before.

Jerry Reinsdorf

I think Chicago fans have had plenty to be upset about as far as the leadership at the top is concerned.

Start off with the Bears. After George Halas died—and to me he was the guy that invented and ran the NFL in its early years—the team was in the hands of Michael McCaskey. I don't think I have to go into details about the way he did his job when the last line on his career history with the Bears is "fired by his own mother."

Bill Wirtz basically ran the Blackhawks into the ground. If you don't think so, look how much Rocky Wirtz has done to make the team relevant again since his father died. "No television broadcast" was his signature, and being cheap was his trademark. He wanted the fans' money, but he didn't want to spend his.

The Cubs have been run by a corporation, and it just hasn't worked out right. They've done fantastic business in terms of interest, but I don't know how good the Tribune Company was at doing its job. But they sure were lucky. They had WGN, and they had Harry Caray. And they didn't screw it up.

But if there has been one owner who has been the right guy for his teams and the right guy for the city of Chicago, it's Jerry Reinsdorf.

He's calm, he's rational, he's smart, and he's a man of his word. He's done right by the Bulls, and he's done right by the Sox. He's won championships with both teams, and I don't think there are too many people in any city who can say they won multiple championships with multiple teams.

> "If there has been one owner who has been the right guy for his teams and the right guy for the city of Chicago, it's Jerry Reinsdorf."

Reinsdorf is a smart guy who hires smart people to run his teams. That's one of the main reasons behind his success. He gets involved in the major decisions. Like the non-hiring of Mike D'Antoni as the Bulls' head coach. Everyone said it was a done deal and that D'Antoni would be the next head coach of the Bulls. But when Reinsdorf talked with him, there were questions—such as D'Antoni's ability to emphasize defense. Reinsdorf didn't get the answer he wanted, and the Bulls went with Vinny Del Negro.

Did he make the right choice? Who knows? When there are major decisions to be made about the direction of the franchise, Reinsdorf is going to be heard from because he wants to feel comfortable about the guy he is hiring—not to tell him how to do his job, but to make sure they are on the same page to begin with.

I think there have been some good owners in sports, but I don't know how you could do much better than Reinsdorf. George Steinbrenner was obviously good for the New York Yankees. When he bought them in the early 1970s, they were basically an irrelevant team, and he was the big reason they were able to come back and become the New York Yankees again. They had basically been forgotten, and they were the second team in New York. People forget that.

The Yankees became a huge business and a juggernaut. You can argue about a lot of the moves that Steinbrenner made, and you can say he brought in players and overpaid them. You can point at any individual move and question it, but the one thing that was obvious about the way Steinbrenner ran the Yankees was that he cared about them, he wanted to win, and he wanted the team to matter again. He knew how to get the attention back on his team, and he knew how to make them important. He may have had a huge ego, but at the end of the day, the Yankees became the dominant team in baseball and maybe in all of sports because of the way he ran his business.

Reinsdorf is pretty similar in that he wants his teams to win, he cares about his teams, and he will make moves to get them better. Of course, Reinsdorf does not have the same kind of interest in being in the headlines every day like Steinbrenner or being on TV every minute, but he is focused on his teams being successful.

Because Reinsdorf doesn't have this huge personality or this need to be on television every minute, some people think he's aloof and not all that friendly. But that's incorrect. He's a regular guy who treats people the right way. He has always treated me pretty well, and my feeling is that Reinsdorf operates by the rule that if somebody treats him honestly and well, he will treat them the same way. He does not put on airs and does not act like he is better than anybody else. You can't ask for more than that from an owner.

He won six championships with the Bulls, but I know that baseball is his true love. That's no secret. He grew up in Brooklyn rooting for the Dodgers, and that's when he fell in love with baseball. Then he got the chance to own a Major League Baseball franchise—not bad for a kid from Brooklyn.

It's interesting that everyone looks at Jerry as the owner of the team, but he really only owns about nine percent of the team. But he's the guy that makes all the key decisions, and that tells you what kind of businessman he is.

In addition to that, he's a good guy. Too bad for the rest of the city the other owners have not done their jobs the way that Reinsdorf has done his. If the Bears had the same kind of leadership that Reinsdorf gives the White Sox and Bulls, I'm sure there would be a lot more than one championship since 1963. The same goes for the Blackhawks. They haven't won since 1961, and while things are getting turned around now, things were going in reverse for way too long. Maybe the Cubs ownership will get straightened out now that Sam Zell finally sold them, but who knows?

Frank Thomas

Frank Thomas had the best batting eye of any player ever to put on a White Sox uniform, and I don't think there's any doubt that he is the most talented hitter in team history.

He was respected by the umpires. He got a lot of calls on close pitches and even got a few when he took a pitch that was right over the middle of the plate. Frank Thomas was born to hit, as evidenced by his place atop the White Sox's leader board in home runs, doubles, slugging percentage, and RBIs.

From the way Thomas started his career, it appeared that he would go down as one of the greatest right-handed hitters in the history of the game. The things he did in his first few years made you think he would end up in a category with Willie Mays, Hank Aaron, and Joe DiMaggio. That's how good he was—that's how talented he was—and he looked to be unstoppable at times.

Of course, Frank didn't quite make it to that level. His numbers are top-drawer, Hall of Fame–type numbers. But he wasn't in a category with Mays, Aaron, or DiMaggio. Much of it was due to injuries that slowed him down. He had a bad ankle, and I'm not sure that he ever recovered fully from that injury. But injuries don't tell the whole story with Frank. I think he could have been a better player had he worked harder. I think he could have been a better player if he had a better attitude.

The most talented hitter in team history, Frank Thomas follows through on a home run against the Seattle Mariners on July 30, 1994, in Chicago. (AP Photo/ John Swart)

Let's get back to that left ankle of his. Thomas underwent surgery to repair a stress fracture of the navicular bone in the fall of 2004 and returned before he was fully healed. He hit .219 with 12 home runs in 105 at-bats that season, but he had to shut it down for good in July 2005. He was never a key part of the White Sox championship run. Yes, he got to throw out the opening pitch of the divisional playoff series and ultimately took part in the World Series parade, but he was never really anything more than a showpiece that year. It's kind of sad that he didn't get to be more active on that team. But the fact of the matter is the White Sox did win the World Series that year, and they did it without him.

If you're Frank Thomas, that really has to hurt. He came up with the team in 1990, and he started playing regularly for them in 1991. He was there when Robin Ventura and Carlton Fisk were there, and he has a real connection to the old-timers.

Thomas would go on to play with Oakland and Toronto and go back to Oakland, but his days with the White Sox came to an end.

That screaming match he had with Kenny Williams really told the story. In the spring of 2006, the two went after each other in the newspapers. For Frank, to open up a list of complaints was almost to be expected. He had left the team and joined the Oakland A's. The White Sox didn't want him anymore, and his feelings were hurt. So he decided to lash out.

"I've got a lot of respect for Jerry Reinsdorf, I do," Thomas said. "But I really thought, the relationship we had over the last 16 years, he would have picked up the phone to say, 'Big guy, we're moving forward. We're going somewhere different. We don't know your situation or what's going to happen.' I can live with that, I really can. But treating me like some passing-by-player. I've got no respect for that"

I guess Williams wasn't going to have any of that. He and Thomas didn't seem to like each other very much, and Williams really didn't have any reason to continue the fight in public other than Thomas had brought up Reinsdorf's name. As a result, Kenny came out firing. He called Thomas an idiot and questioned his manhood.

"If he was any kind of a man, he would quit talking about things in the paper and return a phone call or come knock on someone's door. If I had the kind of problems evidently he had with me, I would go knock on his door," Williams said.

It looked like the two would continue to go back and forth, but Williams decided not to let any personal feelings towards Frank cause any more problems.

The reason I bring this up is because I think it tells you a lot about Thomas and a lot about why his reputation isn't what it should be. Thomas was not an old-school, tough-as-nails ballplayer who only had winning on his mind. I'll tell you what stands out for me and probably a lot of other people, as well. It was that All-Star Game in Texas in 1995.

At the time, Frank was clearly one of the best hitters (if not the best) in the American League. He was representing the American League in the All-Star Game and wearing a White Sox uniform. He hit a home run in that game, one that was really a shot. It was a line drive that might have gone 15–20 rows back, and he just belted it. It was the kind of ball that could have given you whiplash as you watched it leave his bat because it was hit so hard.

When a great player hits a homerun in the All-Star Game and it's the early innings, he should be hungry for more. That's the way Willie Mays, Hank Aaron, and especially Pete Rose were. They didn't want to get in the game and then get out and then take a shower. Guys like that would not want to come out of the game.

But not Frank. After he hit his home run, all he wanted to do was take a shower and get out of there. He didn't care about the game or even getting another at-bat. He was satisfied with hitting a home run and being done for the night.

"After he hit his home run, all he wanted to do was take a shower and get out of there."

That's not the makeup of a great ballplayer. Maybe he had a good reason for getting out of there, but I'll just never swallow it. When you're a great ballplayer and you're honored to be in the starting lineup of the All-Star Game, you live up to that honor and you play for as long as your manager wants you to play. And if he wants to take you out, you should go up to him and ask to be kept in the game. That's how much you should want it.

But that's not Frank Thomas. He wanted out, and he was more interested in doing other things than playing baseball. He had been bothered enough, and he wanted to go.

I think that's a big part of his legacy. Maybe people like me make too much out of it, but I just think someone cares or they don't. And if they don't, they can't pretend they do just when it's convenient.

He has great totals. He's well over 500 home runs. He got a lot of big hits for the White Sox. But as good as he was in that White Sox uniform, I think he could have been better and done more. I don't think I'm alone there. I think a lot of White Sox fans agree with me, and I wouldn't be surprised if Frank Thomas didn't think it was true, as well.

That's too bad. Because however anyone classifies Frank's career—good, very good, excellent, or great—it could have been even better if he had really left it all on the field and played with more fire and passion.

Carlton Fisk

I always thought Carlton Fisk was kind of reserved whenever we had him on the radio show. He was a good guy who tried to answer questions, but I always felt that he was thinking about the reaction that would come from his answer rather than just saying what he thought.

A lot of athletes are that way because they are leery of the press, radio, and television. But most guys will eventually give you an answer somewhere down the road, and I'm not sure Fisk would ever let his guard down.

I give Fisk a lot of credit for being the kind of player he was, and he really brought a lot to the White Sox when he signed with them.

Fisk had a lot of presence and respect around baseball because he was such a hard-working guy. I think that part of his game and his personality really came through when he was with the White Sox, but it was obvious that he was a real hard worker during the first part of his career with the Red Sox. He laid all the groundwork for the success he had in Chicago with what he had done in Boston.

He was clearly a good player in Boston. He won the Rookie of the Year Award, and he had that rivalry with Thurman Munson of the Yankees. They really hated each other, and when you have someone like that in the picture, you always want to show that you are the better player.

I think the thing that really made him a great player was hitting the game-winning home run for the Red Sox in the sixth game of the 1975 World Series. That was as big a game-winning hit as a player could have—with the exception of doing the same thing to win the seventh game. But here was this Red Sox team that was down and out against the great Big Red Machine, and Fisk hit this unbelievable home run to get them to the seventh game.

"I don't know how often he ever talked about how much that hit meant to him."

I don't know how often he ever talked about how much that hit meant to him. Obviously, it won the game for his team and he was the hero, but I've always thought that when a player comes through in such a big spot, it makes him a better player. He has proven to himself that he can come through in the biggest clutch situation, and that means he is a real professional who will not shrink from the moment.

It means a player has got the stones to come through. It gives a guy a lot of respect in the clubhouse, and his presence makes a team that much tougher. I think that's what the White Sox were looking for when they brought him to Chicago, and that's what Fisk had.

I got along fine with Carlton, and he came on the TV show with me. It was a great treat for us because Carlton Fisk was not the type to give a lot of interviews or exclusives, and that's just what we were able to get. Fisk came on with us at Basta Pasta, and there was lot of jealousy from the TV and radio guys because we were able to feature him.

Fisk was quite pleasant, and he answered the questions that we had. He was clearly a no-nonsense kind of player, and that translated into the media and even with his own teammates. He was definitely an old-school kind of guy who would look you in the eye if he didn't understand why a teammate did something or if he didn't like a question. He was direct and I guess some people thought he was abrasive, but I never did.

I think Fisk had as much to do with the White Sox becoming a prominent team and a contender as anyone. When Jerry Reinsdorf and Eddie Einhorn brought him to Chicago, the team was floundering and not really well-thought-of around the American League. They didn't become a good team just because they added Fisk, but he gave them more presence and credibility. With Fisk in the lineup and in the clubhouse, the White Sox got tougher. You had to play a better game to beat them.

You really had to respect the guy for what he did after the game. He never rested on his laurels. Fisk was not the kind of guy who would go 3-for-4 in a game and throw out two guys stealing and then think how great he is and go out and celebrate by drinking three or four beers. No, not Fisk. He would simply go back to work, lift weights, and ride the exercise bike in order to do what he could to stay in shape. It was a perspective that not many ballplayers of his era shared.

Talk about dedicated and hard-working. You know there are a lot of players that will talk a good game and tell you how much baseball means to them and how hard they work. Then you see the guy talking to girls at the bars and staying out late. Fisk wasn't one to say how hard he was going to work or how much he loved the game of baseball. He was an old-school guy who liked to let his actions do the talking. He wasn't interested in what people thought of him—he just wanted to be true to himself and live up to his own standards.

That means so much to a team, especially when you're a player like Fisk who played with the White Sox for such a long time. His teammates saw how he conducted himself, and they eventually learned a few things about how to get the most out of their careers and how to play the game the right way. He didn't have to sit everybody down and explain things to them—he wasn't the type to resort to speechifying anyway. But Fisk's work ethic was present every single day he was in a White Sox uniform.

4

Bulls

Michael Jordan

I never did Michael Jordan justice on the air.

Jordan was the greatest finisher the game has ever seen and probably the second-best player in basketball history. I still think Wilt Chamberlain has a little bit of an edge. I'm not trying to be argumentative or contrary, but that's just how I feel.

Jordan was great and did great things for the Bulls and the city of Chicago. But when he was at his peak, winning championships, MVP awards, and just dominating the game of basketball, I never gave him his due.

In the sports talk radio business, you need something to talk about, and the negative things we say always get much more of a reaction than the positive. That's a given. That's just the way it is for everyone. That's not just the case for Mike North or Dan McNeil or Terry Boers or anyone else, it's just a fact of life. So with Jordan, who was this unbelievable player and great leader for the Bulls, I tended to make more out of the negative stories than the positive ones. Not for any destructive purpose but just because that's the nature of the business and that's human nature as well.

So as the years have gone by since Jordan was in his prime with the Bulls and ultimately winning his last title in 1998, I don't feel

Michael Jordan puts up the game-winning shot over Utah Jazz forward Bryon Russell, right, to win Game 1 of the NBA Finals 84-82 on Sunday, June 1, 1997, in Chicago. (AP Photo/Fred Jewell)

great about the treatment he received. We concentrated on the gambling stories or the rumors of his involvement with other women and maybe not as much as we should have on his actions on the court.

"We concentrated on the gambling stories or the rumors of his involvement with other women and maybe not as much as we should have on his actions on the court."

Jordan was always very nice to me and Be-Be. He was friendly and warm, and when I went to his basketball camp, he busted my chops but it was all in fun, and there was no sense of meanness or anything like that.

Jordan was out of this world as a player and a salesman. He had this ability from the way he carried himself to turn anything he was associated with into gold. From all his Nike endorsements to anything else he ever put his name on, Jordan was just a major success. You know the "Be Like Mike" campaign, well, that's just what the public wanted to do. They wanted to be like Michael Jordan every step of the way, and that kind of popularity is just shocking.

So people who are covering him and talking about him as he is in the midst of this run are going to look for flaws. The advertising world is telling you that he is some kind of basketball god. You know that he is a dominant player, but nothing is ever what it seems so you look for flaws. I guess that's human nature.

As I said, as the years have gone by I don't feel good about it. But the memories of Jordan the basketball player are just unbelievable. When they drafted him in 1984, it seemed like an absolute certainty that they were getting a great player. But who knew how great he was going to be? It was clear during his rookie season that he would soon be one of the greatest players in the game, and that was at a time when Magic Johnson and Larry Bird were still flying high.

Jordan handled himself with a lot of dignity in the early stages of his career. I think that's why a lot of people noticed him. Yes, he could dominate a game and take over because of his great athletic ability, but I think what really impressed people is that he seemed almost humble when he would talk about what he had done after a game. He wasn't bragging, and he seemed sincere. People like that, and that's what touched a nerve with sports fans in Chicago, the country, and ultimately around the world. It was the likability factor with Jordan. Very few superstars have that. There always seems to be some amount of "I'm better than you are" in an athlete's attitude. Jordan believed that and showed that with his play on the floor, and I think that's what gave him the extra fire that allowed him to become as great as he was. But after the game and off the floor, most people thought that if they were having a beer with Michael Jordan or having a sandwich with him—make it an Italian Beef with extra juice and hot peppers—it would be a positive experience.

One of the greatest memories as far as I'm concerned was that first championship. He had wanted it so badly from the time he entered the league, and it was clear that winning was his primary goal. The way he would take over games and dominate from a scoring perspective was not about getting him the glory and the adulation but about helping the Bulls to win. A lot of athletes say they want to win but really couldn't care less as long as they get the money and the glory. This was not Jordan. He wanted to win.

So when the Bulls got past the Pistons in four straight—and I will never, ever get over the classless move of the Pistons walking off the court after the Bulls swept them—they were a team that was on edge. They were so close to their first championship and title that they could taste it. Losing the first game enhanced the nervousness and the determination. They were as ready to play as any team could be, and when they took the floor for the second game, they were ready to dominate. That was the game where Jordan went in for the layup and switched the ball from his right hand to his left hand in mid-air while laying the ball up. It became one of the staples in Jordan's highlight reel, but in reality it was even more than that. It was that play in the middle of a Bulls blowout that told the rest of the basketball world that the Bulls were the better team and in charge of the series.

They proved it when they went out to Los Angeles and swept the Lakers in three games. Jordan's kick-out pass to John Paxson in the closing stages of the fourth quarter was more than just the finishing touch on the series. It was also when he demonstrated that he knew that getting his teammates involved would make the team even stronger. The Bulls had shown for a while that they were not a one-man team, but when Jordan showed he was willing to pass up open shots to his teammates, it sent a message to the rest of the league that nobody was going to be able to beat the Bulls in any games of any consequence for quite a long time.

That was the beginning of Jordan's dominance as a *team* player. He started to dominate individually from the minute the Bulls drafted him, but there's some irony that Rod Thorn, the Bulls' general manager at the time, refused to go overboard in his analysis of the player he brought to Chicago with the third pick in the NBA draft. Thorn said that he thought Jordan would be a very good scorer but "not an overpowering offensive force."

Thorn probably rethought that last statement over the years. Jordan led the league in scoring a record 10 times, and in 1986–87 became the only player besides Chamberlain to score more than 3,000 points in a season, netting 3,041.

Jordan won the regular-season MVP five times and the Finals MVP six times. In 1991 and 1992, he became the only player to win back-to-back regular season and Finals MVP awards, and in 1993 he became the first to win the Finals MVP three consecutive years, a feat he repeated from 1996–98.

If Jordan showed the fire in the Bulls' first championship run, he still had it during their last championship drive in 1998 against Utah. Not only was that last shot over Bryon Russell probably the most famous moment in Jordan's career, but it came after he had taken the ball away from Karl Malone and was the last score of a 45-point night. It was perhaps his greatest game ever in a Bulls uniform, at least as a team player.

The greatest game of his career came in the 1986 playoffs against the Boston Celtics. Jordan had missed most of the season with a broken foot and probably had 10 times as much energy as anyone on the court as a result. The Celtics had the better team with Larry Bird, Kevin McHale, and Robert Parish, but it was clear that Jordan was not going to get down on his knees and worship the Celtics. Instead, he just hit every shot imaginable and scored 63 points on the parquet floor at the old Boston Garden. It was the first time he went past the 50-point mark in his career. The Celtics would win the game in overtime, but Jordan's performance led to a thoughtful assessment by Bird after the game, "That wasn't Michael Jordan on the floor. That was God disguised as Michael Jordan."

 "'That wasn't Michael Jordan on the floor. That was God disguised as Michael Jordan.'"

When looking at Jordan's career, the basic assessment is that he had remarkable athletic ability coupled with this unbelievable competitive fire. I pretty much agree with that, but let's take it a step further. Here's what I think made Jordan the player that he became:

COMPETITIVENESS

The idea of going on the basketball court and taking on anyone and anything in his way. He wanted to win, of course, but more than that, he just wanted to go out there and compete. He wanted to assess the competition and of course beat them. Jordan would come out and take the measure of whichever team was in the other uniform and develop a plan of attack. There was a team game plan and then there was the Jordan game plan that would be developed based on how he felt and who the opponent was.

HATING TO LOSE

Remember the Bad Boys of Detroit? Chicago fans hated Bill Laimbeer, Rick Mahorn, Dennis Rodman, Joe Dumars, and Isiah Thomas. They were a tough, physical team that basically beat up the Bulls as they beat them. If Jordan didn't hate losing before the Bulls dropped those NBA playoff series to the Pistons, he did as Detroit imposed the Jordan Rules on the Bulls and beat them three series in a row. Everybody hates losing, but nobody hated losing more than Jordan. Especially to that little bastard Thomas. That evil grin on his face. Nothing was better than seeing that guy walk off the court like the spoiled brat he was. Couldn't even bear to shake hands after the series. No class.

RESILIENCY

You remember Jordan coming back from his first retirement? Of course, he wanted to give baseball a try, and once he realized that wasn't going to work, he came back to the Bulls. They lost in the playoffs that year, and Jordan knew he wasn't at his best. Critics were quick to question his heart and his reasons for coming back. They said it would be nearly impossible for Michael to regain his dominance. He took that criticism to heart and worked on all aspects of his game—mental, physical, and emotional—to go on and play sensational basketball once again.

CLUTCH PLAY

Jordan showed who he would become in college when he hit the NCAA Championship winning shot for North Carolina over Georgetown in 1982. At the pro level, the start of his great clutch play came as he hit the series-winning shot over Craig Ehlo so the Bulls beat the Cleveland Cavaliers. After that, Jordan had that air of inevitability about him. It seemed like he would hit every clutch shot that came his way, and it was almost a surprise if he even missed one.

JORDAN'S 10 GREATEST BULLS MOMENTS

10. **I can do anything better than you—April 16, 1987.** Jordan scored 61 points against Dominique Wilkins and the Hawks. It was a game the Bulls lost but one where Jordan showed he took it personally.

9. **The comeback—March 28, 1995.** Jordan scored 55 points in his fifth game back following his 18-month retirement from basketball. He did it against the Knicks in Madison Square Garden while wearing the No. 45 on the back of his uniform.

8. **Ehlo's nightmare—May 7, 1989.** Jordan hit a series-winning 15-footer over Craig Ehlo to give the Bulls the series. The Cavs would never be the same after that series, which proved that Jordan and the Bulls were going up.

7. **Food poisoning—June 11, 1997.** Game 5 of the finals. Jordan supposedly ate some bad pizza and looked like he should be in the hospital. Even though he appeared to be on the verge of collapse, Jordan scored 38 and the Bulls were one game away from their fifth title.

6. **Celtic mystique—April 20, 1986.** Jordan went into the Boston Garden against Larry Bird, Kevin McHale, and Robert Parrish and

delivered 63 points in a losing playoff game. The game told the rest of the NBA that Jordan was fearless in all situations.

5. **The layup—June 5, 1991.** After losing the first game of the NBA Finals, Jordan led the Bulls to a blowout win in Game 2, with his midair switch from right hand to left while making a layup being the highlight of the series.

4. **Career-high—March 28, 1990.** Jordan went after his nemesis, the Cavs, once again. He scored a career-high 69 points and also threw in 18 rebounds for good measure.

3. **Championship delivered—June 12, 1991.** The Bulls won the fifth game of the Finals against the Lakers, and Jordan sat on the floor of the locker room crying and making love to the Larry O'Brien Trophy—and sharing the moment with his father.

2. **The shoulder shrug—June 3, 1992.** It was the first game of the NBA finals and Jordan welcomed the Portland Trail Blazers to the party by scoring 35 points in the first half and hitting six three-pointers. After the last of those three-pointers, Jordan shrugged his shoulders as if to say, "I can't believe it either."

1. **Say good night—June 14, 1998.** The push off and the shot over Bryon Russell gave the Bulls their sixth NBA title. Remember Jordan holding his form after he let the ball go, emphasizing that it was the last moment of his Bulls career. That's how to say good-bye. Too bad he had to come back with the Wizards, but that night was his NBA signature.

Phil Jackson

Phil Jackson is the great basketball genius of our time. That's what Big Chief Triangle would have you believe.

Here's the truth: Phil Jackson is the great basketball genius of his own mind.

To me, he's a decent coach. He's also about the luckiest guy to ever serve as a coach or manager of any major sport.

Think about it—he became head coach of the Bulls at a time when they were about to mature into a great team. They had Michael Jordan, the best player of his time. They had Scottie Pippen and Horace Grant. They had John Paxson. Tell me, what exactly did Jackson do except go along for the ride?

"Phil Jackson is the great basketball genius of his own mind."

He came along at a point when Jordan was starting to understand how important team play was. Maybe Jackson helped that process, but how much help did Miller Huggins have to give Babe Ruth? How much help did Jim Brown need from Paul Brown and Blanton Collier? Did Glen Sather have to give Wayne Gretzky special instructions in order to make The Great One even better? Not likely.

Jordan was a phenomenon of a player who could basically take over any game whenever he wanted to. He could do it all—dribble, pass, shoot, and defend—and he was at the point where he was using those skills. If he was double-teamed or triple-teamed, he knew how to get the ball to the open man.

So why is Jackson such a great coach? He was smart enough to coach the second-greatest player of all time when he was at his absolute peak? That's a real skill? I would call that lucky.

Then Jackson went to Los Angeles and he had Shaquille O'Neal and Kobe Bryant. Having those guys makes a coach look awfully smart.

He has nine titles just like Red Auerbach. Are you going to tell me that Jackson is even close to the same kind of coach as Auerbach? That's not going to work. Auerbach drafted, coached, and worked game plans for every championship his teams won. He did it with-

When Michael Jordan was on your team, how good of a coach did you really need to be? Here, Phil Jackson and Jordan talk during a timeout in their Eastern Conference Final game on Saturday, May 25, 1996, in Orlando. (AP Photo/Steve Simoneau)

out offensive superstars. Auerbach's Celtics played team basketball because they had to. Bill Russell, John Havlicek, and Bob Cousy— that kind of team didn't have the great talent that the Bulls did, so Auerbach had to outthink the coaches on the other bench.

Of course, Jackson liked to think of himself as some kind of genius with all of his off-the-court interests. Passing out books on the road to his players. Give me a break. Like that had anything to do with the Bulls winning. That is the most ridiculous thing I've ever heard. Jackson was so lucky to have Jordan and others on the team who seemed amused by this and the other stunts that Jackson pulled. If Jordan wasn't on the team and giving Jackson the stamp of approval, players would not have listened. I have nothing against books—hell, I'm writing this one—but if you think for one instant I'm going to read a book because Phil Jackson has "specifically picked it out" for me, you've got another thing coming. Maybe I'd use it for a paperweight or something like that, but I'd have no use for it in any other situation.

And even the triangle offense. I'll give Jackson credit for one thing: he had Tex Winter on hand to teach that offense and help run it. I'm not so sure that the triangle is the be-all and end-all, but it was by no means Jackson's baby. He had Winter to teach it to the team and perfect it in practice. That was Jerry Krause's doing. He's a guy who's easy to pick on because he's short and dumpy, but he was very good at his job. He brought in Bill Cartwright, and he wasn't afraid to sign Dennis Rodman. So it has to mean something when you have a guy who can bring in the right pieces. Sure, Jordan was the biggest part of the deal, and Krause wasn't the one who brought him in. But at least he brought in some key pieces, and you can make an argument that he had as much or more to do with the team's success as Jackson.

That would be tough for Jackson or Jordan to swallow, but it does have some truth and validity to it.

Here's another thing about Jackson: he didn't exactly stick around after the second three-peat. Scottie Pippen wanted more money, and Michael Jordan was going to retire. So Jackson wanted to get out of there as quick as possible. Is that really what great coaches do? Don't they stay around when there is some difficulty and try to show just what kind of coaches they are? Or do they cut and run when it gets difficult in order to preserve their reputations? That's not what it's supposed to be all about. You should want to fight if you have any stones. You want to be able to win with a great team and at least compete with a team that isn't so great. You can really respect a coach who is not afraid to fight when the situation gets a bit ugly. But Jackson wanted no part of it.

Jackson seemed very predictable in the way he dealt with the Bulls' front office. Jackson used his pull with his players to hold up the club on an annual basis as he "considered" his future. Since he was Jordan's guy, he had that kind of power. Jackson used that relationship to improve his own situation, and nobody can tell me he didn't want Krause out of there so he could make all the team's personnel decisions.

Did Jackson do what anyone who had established credentials as one of the NBA's best coaches ever, who wanted to grow in influence beyond mere coaching, would do? Of course. But in the process of helping to prematurely end the Bulls' championship run and then refusing to take less-assured situations with a score of teams that offered full control and open bank vaults, Jackson unwittingly undermined his own coaching legacy.

When he got back into coaching, it was with the Lakers, a team nearly as loaded with talent as the Bulls. He had to do some coaching to get Shaq and Kobe to play well with each other and he got three more championships, but it wasn't like he could keep those guys together. It disappeared for a while, but the Lakers came back in 2007–08 and got to the Finals.

If Jackson was really such a genius, why did he have to come back to such a loaded team? What was that all about? If you want to show you have some ability and that you can really be a great coach, then take a team like the Memphis F---ing Grizzlies and win a championship with them. Then you're a great coach. But when you win with Michael and you win with Shaq and Kobe, the only thing you are doing is not screwing up a situation that you should win.

The "genius" was about to break the NBA record for titles and do it against the Celtics. But a funny thing happened on his way to the title. They lost to the Celtics, and Jackson had to taste championship defeat. Not only did the Lakers lose the sixth and final game after playing a relatively good series, but they got absolutely destroyed in the sixth game by almost 40 points (131–92). They had all the toughness of an overcooked marshmallow when all the money was on the table. They fell apart.

 "If you want to show you have some ability and that you can really be a great coach, then take a team like the Memphis F---ing Grizzlies and win a championship with them."

The team had set the tone for what would happen in the fourth game. That was back in Los Angeles, and the Lakers had won Game 3 to cut the deficit to 2–1. They broke out to a 35–14 lead and looked like they were going to blow the Celtics out of the Staples Center, but they just didn't have what they needed to finish the job. You get that kind of lead in a game in your building in the Finals, and you are supposed to get the job done. But the Celtics wouldn't go away. They had a huge run (21–3) in the third quarter, and their bench showed much more desire than anyone on the Lakers bench. You're supposed to have some toughness when you're in that situation, but they had none of it. That was a display of weak stock and, of course, they were going to fold up when they went back to Boston.

So Jackson's supposed to be such a great coach and the best of all-time. Not in my book and not even close.

Scottie Pippen

It's hard to imagine anyone having a more wide-ranging career than Scottie Pippen. Here's a guy who nobody ever heard of who made a name for himself at the Portsmouth Invitational Tournament against other rookies and raised his draft status.

He was drafted by Seattle, and the Bulls traded for him on Draft Day. He went on to become the No. 2 guy on the Bulls to Jordan's No.

1, and he won six titles along the way. An All-Star multiple times, Pippen had a great career by any way you want to measure it. Yet there was something missing for him. He played in Jordan's shadow for such a long time that he ended up resenting it. He wanted to be the No. 1 guy, but he never could.

Scottie Pippen stuffs one in the second period of the Chicago Bulls 115–92 victory over the Golden State Warriors at the San Jose Arena in San Jose on Friday, January 31, 1997. Pippen scored 32 points. (AP Photo/Susan Ragan)

Well, check that. He was the No. 1 guy during Jordan's first retirement. How did that go for him? The Bulls didn't win championships with Pippen as the No. 1 guy, and they didn't win too many playoff series. When Jordan came back, they three-peated again. I'm sure Pippen was happy to win three titles in a row on two different occasions, but I'm just as sure that there was something that ate at him and bothered him because he wasn't the No. 1 guy. That was clear from the way he carried himself and the way he acted.

And that's pretty sad. Because look at where he came from. He went to the University of Central Arkansas, of all places, and it's a pretty good leap from there to the NBA. He wasn't even a scholarship player when he got there because he was this awkward guy who had size going for him but little else. Pippin posted 4.3 ppg in his first season there, but he got better throughout his career, and by the time he finished his senior year, he was averaging 23.6 ppg. He was a guy who the Bulls worked into the lineup slowly along with Horace Grant, and once he got it going, he was a great all-around player. By the end of his rookie year, the Bulls were back in the playoffs. When they played Cleveland in the playoffs, Pippin was a key member of the rotation and he was a starter before the end of the series. Then he started in a losing playoff series against Detroit.

Scottie could handle the ball, he could run like a gazelle, and he could play defense. Oh, what a defensive player. He had these long arms and long legs, and he could get into those passing lanes and cause havoc. He was a great offensive player who could finish on the break and hit the outside shot. He was an outstanding player anyway you want to look at it. But he was not the No. 1 guy, and the more time that went by the more difficult it was for him to accept it.

Pippin's rise up the ladder was really an incredible story. He was a solid player in his second year and an All-Star by his third year. That was Phil Jackson's first year as head coach, and that's when

Tex Winter installed the triangle offense. Who was better at filling lanes, stealing the ball, and getting the fast break going than Pippen? Well, Jordan was better, but once again it was Pippen filling the No. 2 role.

It's hard to believe a player who averaged single-digit scoring at Central Arkansas could rise to such heights—and have a problem with it. But there was always so much that bothered the guy and it really looked like everything fell apart for him in the 1994 playoffs. That's when there were 1.8 seconds left in the playoff game with the Knicks, Jackson called a play for Toni Kukoc and Pippen went berserk and opted out of the play.

"It's hard to believe a player who averaged single-digit scoring at Central Arkansas could rise to such heights—and have a problem with it."

How could anyone do that? He waited so long to get his opportunity and then it finally came as Jordan had retired for the first time. So on this play, the Bulls were tied but had a chance to hit the game-winning shot. They had to win because they were down 2–0, and he just lost it when Jackson gave the shot to Kukoc.

Kukoc, of course, hit that game winner. But it didn't matter to Pippen. This was supposed to be his opportunity. He had said that with Jordan retired, he would lead the Bulls to the championship. How could he do this if Jackson was giving the shot to Kukoc of all people?

Pippen's teammates were shocked by the move, which has to go down as one of the most selfish of all time. "I was shocked," Steve Kerr later admitted. "The only way to describe it was total disbelief. Here was a guy who had done so much for our team, who had been our leader all year long. He was, and still is, one of the greatest teammates I've ever had. But on that day, I think all the pressure and frustration of our season caught up with him, and he snapped."

Here's how it went down: Jackson called his team into the huddle and diagrammed the final shot for Kukoc. Pippen, who wanted the chance to win the game himself, was shocked and angry to learn that he was going to be relegated to inbounding the ball. He swore at his coach, stomped out of the huddle, and stormed down to the end of the bench, leaving his team in the lurch for the most important moment of the game—and perhaps of the Bulls' season.

Kukoc hit a fall-away 23-footer. Still, Jackson, a coach known for protecting his players at all costs, didn't even try to conceal his feelings of betrayal. As he walked into the interview room, he announced unprovoked, "Scottie asked out of the play."

After Jackson made that announcement, everybody went nuts. All anyone could talk about on the air was what Pippen did and how awful it was. He was a traitor for that mistake, and we were not about to forgive him.

The reaction was not much better for Pippen around the rest of the country than it was in Chicago. Nobody could even think of anyone pulling any kind of similar behavior. The fact that the Bulls won the game did not make it any easier for Pippen. People were going after him with all guns blazing.

I guess the only one who felt even a little sorry for him was Jordan. He said he felt bad for Pippen and had warned him how hard it was to be the leader. Nobody thought Pippen would ever be able to turn things around after becoming the poster child for self-centered behavior on the basketball court.

But a few days later, Pippen probably helped himself. He apologized to his teammates, and he apologized to Jackson. He came back and had a great game as the Bulls won the fourth game to tie the series, but the Bulls lost the series in seven games. His selfish and destructive behavior destroyed his credibility as the leader he wanted to be. He probably never would have been able to rescue his career if Jordan had not decided to come back from his first retirement.

Once Jordan did come back, it gave Pippen a chance to rescue his reputation and continue to improve as a ballplayer. Jordan once again handled all the prime-time scoring and was as good as he had ever been before his first retirement. Meanwhile, Scottie became very creative on both the offensive and defensive ends. The incident was never going to be forgotten, but it became part of his history. Everyone knew it was there, but it was no longer the only thing people talked about when the subject was Pippen. At least it wasn't the first thing they talked about.

Pippen became a much happier person and more comfortable in his role with the Bulls. After the Bulls won the title in 1995–96, they got on another roll. It was clear they were going to win the next year, and Pippen enjoyed what he was doing as Jordan's partner in crime, even if he was still the junior partner. "Michael and I have a sense that when the other isn't going well that it's time to step up," Pippen said. "When he's going well, I want the ball in his hands. I know sooner or later that he will create chances for others."

The Bulls went on to win their sixth title, and that was it for Jordan. And that was it for the Bulls, as well. Pippen had made it clear that he wanted a big free-agent contract and that he didn't want it to be with the Bulls. Pippen left, Jackson left, and Jordan retired. It was suddenly all over.

Pippen went on to play with the Rockets, Blazers, and even returned briefly to the Bulls. But he would never win a title in any of those other stops, and that meant he never won a title without Jordan.

That doesn't take away from Pippen's career because it was a great one. However, it seemed that it ate at him, and he was the one player who didn't get as much enjoyment as he should have.

Dennis Rodman

Lipstick, nail polish, outrageous hair colors, and wedding dresses: that's how a lot of people think of Dennis Rodman. Is he some kind of kook? Of course. But when he was in a Bulls uniform and the Bulls were in the playoffs, he was a formidable player.

I think he should be in the Hall of Fame. I think it's a crime that he's not in the Hall of Fame. Because for all of his histrionics and despite the ruckus that he caused, he was a big reason why the Bulls were able to get that second three-peat.

"I think it's a crime that he's not in the Hall of Fame."

He was just a rebounding machine. He was the best pound-for-pound rebounder the game has ever seen, and that includes Bill Russell and Wilt Chamberlain and anyone else who ever played the game. And I loved Chamberlain—he was the best player who ever walked on an NBA court. But when it came to rebounding, nobody got more out of himself or gave more of himself to the game than Rodman.

He was a great fit for the Bulls. It was a great get by Jerry Krause. To bring him in and take the chance could have been a disaster, but Krause saw the upside. Jordan knew just how to treat Rodman. He knew when to buddy up to him and when to lay down the law. When Scottie Pippen and Rodman were both playing defense, it was almost impossible to work a play against the Bulls. And even Phil Jackson figured out the right rotation to use Rodman.

It was a great marriage, and it was no coincidence that the Bulls set the league record for wins and won three straight titles for a second time when they had Rodman.

Dennis Rodman should be in the Hall of Fame. Here, Rodman grabs a rebound during the second quarter of the Bulls 87–82 defeat of the Charlotte Hornets on Saturday, December 14, 1996, in Chicago. Rodman returned from a two-game suspension and brought down a season-high 23 rebounds. (AP Photo/Tim Boyle)

In 14 seasons, Rodman averaged 7.3 points and 13.1 rebounds. For seven consecutive years, he led the league in rebounding—an NBA record.

Only Wilt Chamberlain, with 11, won more rebounding titles than Rodman, who played for five championship teams and appeared in two All-Star Games. Twice the league's defensive player of the year, Rodman made the all-defensive first team seven times.

But it was his play when the championship was on the line that made him a Hall of Fame player. Throughout the whole of his career, Karl Malone was basically an unstoppable offensive player, but what happened when he played against the Bulls in two championship series? He had a couple of good games, but he lost the ability to score consistently. In the 1998 finals, Malone came through with 39 points in Game 5. That was the game where the Bulls were supposed to clinch the title, but the Jazz came back and won that game in Chicago when they had been trailing 3–1. But the game before that, when it was still a competitive series, Rodman shut down Malone and didn't allow him to get the ball down low and score.

Then in the sixth game back in Utah, when the Jazz were supposed to exert their dominance and get back in the series, Rodman didn't let that happen. That game will always be remembered for Jordan hitting his last shot with the Bulls to give the Bulls the win, but would he have had that chance if Rodman hadn't been playing that kind of defense against Malone? I don't think so.

The guy hustled all over the court. He could have been much more of a scorer if that's what he had concentrated on. He was not interested in taking 15-foot or 20-foot shots. He was interested in getting rebounds and playing defense. A lot of superstars around basketball don't want to do those jobs because they are hard. It's considered dirty work, and a lot of players want to concentrate on putting up great offensive numbers. They can all talk a good game about playing defense and playing "team" basketball, and it's really just so much bullshit because a lot of players couldn't care less.

Then you look at Rodman. When he's in the locker room and when he's outside of the court, everything about his personality is saying, "Look at me," and "Point your cameras at the money." It was all about dating Madonna and marrying Carmen Electra and living the good life and partying. But go back to the court and look at what the guy did.

He played hard. He fought for every rebound he ever got, and he was a winner. Bulls fans hated Rodman when he was in a Detroit uniform, but once he came here and played for about two or three weeks, it was clear that he was going to help the Bulls get back to being a championship team. Remember, the Bulls had a year without Jordan, and when he came back the next year, they lost a playoff series.

The Bulls needed some help, and Krause made the move and brought in Rodman. It was brilliant. He fit right in on the court. He was not best friends with anybody on the team, but he fit in on the court, he made the Bulls a better team, and he helped them win those last three championships.

As far as all the other stuff goes, I was always amused by Rodman. He shouldn't have kicked that camera man in the nuts up in Minnesota, but that was pretty much the exception. Showing up in a wedding dress to sign books? That's just great self-promotion. The outfits, the chains, the leather…why would any Bulls fans give a rat's ass about what this guys was going to do off the court? All that mattered was how he played. If he wanted to bring attention to himself once the game was over, more power to him. And I think he did pretty well. The cameras followed the guy around, he got parts in movies, and he took advantage of his fame. That's fine. He helped the Bulls win championships. He got rebounds, and he helped shut down Malone. He was a winner for the Bulls, and they should be very glad he was here.

5

Blackhawks

Bobby Hull

I have seen all the great athletes in Chicago and all the great players. I've seen Walter Payton at his best and Dick Butkus at his most ferocious. I've seen Michael Jordan take control of nearly every playoff series he ever played in with more ability in his pinkie than just about everybody else who has played the game. I've seen Carlton Fisk catch in the major leagues for more than two decades, and I've watched Ferguson Jenkins pitch for the Cubs.

There have been so many great performers in this city but I can't say that I've ever seen anybody better or more dominant than Bobby Hull. When he was flying high in the 1960s and early '70s with the No. 9 uniform, his great speed, and unbelievable shot, he was one of the most memorable athletes I ever saw in person.

 "There have been so many great performers in this city but I can't say that I've ever seen anybody better or more dominant than Bobby Hull."

The Chicago Stadium crowd roared when he would get the puck. It's still so clear. You can remember him coming from his own end, getting

Bobby Hull (9) skates down the ice with the puck during a hockey game against the Boston Bruins in Chicago on January 7, 1968. Hull scored the 400th and 401st goals of his career during the game. Blackhawks won 4-2. (AP Photo)

a pass from Stan Mikita or one of the defenseman, and picking up speed as he flew down the left side—it just took your breath away. Watching him skate with the puck was one thing, but then watching him wind up and deliver the hardest shot that anyone has ever seen was just unbelievable. He carried the Blackhawks when he was at his best, and his performance dominated the league.

I don't care what the so-called experts say. I think most of them would laugh and try to pat you on the head if you told them that Hull was the best hockey player ever. They would try to dismiss that thought and bring up Wayne Gretzky. Some other misguided hockey writers and fans might bring up Bobby Orr.

They might have plenty of statistics on their side, but I would never say that Gretzky or Orr were better than Hull. I'm talking about when he was his most dominant. I remember the year Phil Esposito scored 76 goals for the Boston Bruins. No doubt he was exactly what that team needed, and he was a good player. Remember, he was a Blackhawk before he made it big with the Bruins. But those 76 goals he scored, they were all rebounds, deflections, short shots, and back-handers. I think they were probably an average of 5 feet each.

When Hull scored 58 goals in 1968–69, it was because he was just unstoppable when he was shooting the puck. These were not tip-ins, deflections, or rebounds at the edge of the crease. Not that there's anything wrong with that, as they would say on *Seinfeld*. Believe me, I wish the Blackhawks had more guys on their current team who could handle the puck around the net, convert those rebounds, deflect the point shots, and put it in. But are you going to tell me there was anything more spectacular that watching Bobby Hull in full flight take the puck from his own zone, move it all the way up ice, and then blast a slap shot?

To actually see this in person was almost shocking. I'm telling you that when Bobby would let go of a slap shot, the opposing goalies were absolutely shaking in their skates. This was the era when some goalies were wearing masks and some were not. There were definitely more goalies wearing masks each season than the one before, but how in the world was it possible for these guys to play against Hull knowing that his shot was going to reach 120 miles per hour? That was absolutely insane.

To watch that slap shot blow by the goalie and explode into the net is one of the best things any sports fan could see. But here's what shocked me the most: it was the sound the puck would make when one of Hull's shots hit the post or crossbar. That's a loud and very unusual sound no matter who is doing the shooting. When a shot comes in from the point on a power play, it's going to have a lot of speed and power. But when one of Hull's shots hit the post, it was like the sound of a shotgun blast. It was so loud and so unusual that it was like, "What just happened?"

I can't give Gretzky the edge over Hull no matter how many goals and points he had. Gretzky was very creative, a great passer, and always in the right place at the right time. I'm not attacking him, and I never would. Hull may have been the strongest guy I ever saw on the ice. If he wanted to, he could overwhelm the opposition physically. He was big, he was strong, and he was tough. If he wanted to fight, he could feed anyone their lunch and throw a beating with the best of them. As the years went by, he fought less and less, but nobody messed with him. He was too strong. Gretzky had bodyguards and guys who would protect him because he was so skinny. That's just the way it was, and it's not his fault that he was not a physically dominant player. But the game of hockey is about more than making the pretty pass. It's about being strong and physical. So how do you call anyone who wasn't going to be physical the best player ever? As far as I'm concerned, the argument ends right there.

The other guy? Orr? It's hard to say anything against him, and I know that Hull held him in very high regard, as did anybody who ever played him. He had incredible speed, he could handle the puck, and he was one of these athletes who saw the game three or four steps ahead and would make the crowds in Boston think about him the same way we thought about Hull.

Hull once said that when Orr was playing, two pucks should be used in the game. "One for Orr and one for the rest of us," Hull said. So I'm not going to say anything about Orr other than injuries kept him from being even greater, and that's just the way it was. He really was not at his peak for as long as some of the others, and that's too bad for him, the Bruins, and all the fans of the sport. Hull was healthier longer, and that has to count for something.

Hull and Mikita were the guys who might have done more to make the game exciting than anyone else. Those guys introduced the curved stick to the NHL, and when Hull wound up for a slap shot and let it fly at full strength, not only would it approach 110 or 120 miles per hour, it would curve or dip or maybe even rise a little bit. I don't know how any of the goaltenders hung in against that kind of shot. And they did it *without* a mask.

> "Hull and Mikita were the guys who might have done more to make the game exciting than anyone else."

I guess there were other goalies who went without masks against that shot, but the guy I remember seeing was Eddie Giacomin of the New York Rangers. I think he was one of the last guys in the league to ever put on a mask in something like 1970–71. But that meant for five or six years, he was playing goal for the Rangers and facing Hull's shot without a mask. At that time, there were just six teams in the league, and that meant the Hawks and Rangers played 14 times a year. Can you imagine facing Hull's slap shot with that curve on the stick that many times a year? I remember looking at Giacomin's face before the game or during a timeout. He didn't look particularly scared, but he didn't look very happy, either. How could he?

Hull was such a crowd pleaser and such a big star that I think it might have taken a little bit away from Mikita. He was a great player in his own right. He was a great center who would win the face off, carry the puck up ice, make the pass, and also had a blistering shot of his own. Not just a slap shot, Mikita had a great wrist shot—a backhander—and he could do from all angles. Maybe he wasn't Hull, but he was a great player, and he gave the Hawks a tremendous one-two punch. To think that the team only won one Stanley Cup is just unbelievable. I mean, who was better than Hull and Mikita? They should have won two or three more.

There's so much talk about Chicago being a Bears town, or a Cubs town, or maybe even a Bulls town when Jordan was winning six championships in the 1990s. But true Chicago sports fans remember that when the Blackhawks were flying and the Chicago Stadium was full and roaring every night and Hull was letting that shot go at full steam and in full stride, Chicago was a hockey town first and foremost.

That's not the case anymore. Maybe things are starting to turn around with a new regime running the show, but Chicago lost a lot of its passion for the game when Bill Wirtz did not re-sign Hull and he ended up going to the Winnipeg Jets of the World Hockey Association. How do you not bring back Bobby Hull? That question could never be answered to any hockey fan's satisfaction, and there's no doubt that's what triggered the downturn in hockey in Chicago. Fans have always responded when the Hawks have been good or even in the playoffs, but there has never been anything close to the excitement surrounding the team that there was when Hull was wearing No. 9 and flying up and down the Chicago Stadium ice.

How could there be? He was the greatest hockey player to ever put on a Chicago Blackhawks uniform, and he was the greatest player ever.

Blackhawks on the Move

They're on their way and they have made great strides, but can the Blackhawks ever recapture the city the way they once owned it?

I think they are on the right road. I think they have a real chance to get back to the days of Bobby Hull and Stan Mikita in the 1960s and '70s when they made the fans in the Stadium roar every time they took the ice. To understand where the Hawks are going you really have to understand where they have been. I'm not exaggerating when I say that they had the city in the palm of their hands in those days. Everybody wanted tickets, and everybody wanted to go to the Stadium.

It was just a major event. Hull was the guy everybody wanted to see because he could just absolutely fly up and down the ice and when he shot the puck, well, I don't think there's ever been anyone else who could shoot it as hard as Bobby Hull. Not his son Brett, not Gordie Howe, not Bobby Orr, and certainly not Wayne Gretzky. Hull had the hardest slap shot of them all, and I don't think you can make a case for anybody else.

Mikita was just a great all-around player who could do it all. He'd make the perfect pass. His shot was as accurate as could be. He'd win the faceoff, and of course, he could handle himself back in the day. The Hawks had those two guys in Hull and Mikita to be their leaders and they had a great supporting cast.

The team is building toward the same thing once again. I think those two kids Patrick Kane and Jonathan Toews are the current version of Hull and Mikita. I'm not saying that they are as good as those two because they are so young and they have so much they still need to accomplish. They have a lot of work to do, but they are headed in the right direction.

 "I think those two kids Patrick Kane and Jonathan Toews are the current version of Hull and Mikita."

Let's face it, this team went absolutely nowhere for the last 15 years or so before Bill Wirtz died. He was an outstanding business-man, and he was a charitable guy, and he did right by his family. But he didn't do right by his team or the fans. I know he didn't like me being critical of him, but that's too bad. He earned that criticism with the way he ran the team. The policy of not putting the home games on television set the franchise back for years, and they didn't do anything to build the fan base. It was just the same thing year after year. It was a stale product.

Wirtz didn't want to spend money to make the team better, either. If there were big free-agents to bring in I don't think he wanted to pay to get the top level players. Sure, he might have brought in one or two guys here or there, but the Hawks weren't considered players in the National Hockey League. They became an afterthought in their own sport, and they became an afterthought in their own city. It was just unbelievable because once upon a time this franchise *owned* the city of Chicago.

I can give you the exact moment that things started to turn bad for the Hawks. It's a pretty obvious one: when Hull left to play in the World Hockey Association in Winnipeg, of all places, that started the downhill slide. It wasn't really a slide, either. It was more like a downhill avalanche.

How could the Blackhawks not bring him back? I don't care how much he cost or what they would have had to do to keep him. Bobby Hull was the Blackhawks, and the Blackhawks were Bobby Hull. To have him go to another league and wear another uniform was complete crap. He was a Blackhawk. He should have always been a Blackhawk, and he never should have left. How Bill Wirtz didn't know that was unbelievable. It was his team, and if you wanted to look at it from a business sense, Hull was his absolute best asset. You can't let your assets disappear for nothing.

The fans resented it, and they were angry for a long time. And one other thing: the team simply was not as good as it had been. People began to lose interest.

To me, letting go of Bobby Hull was the second-biggest bonehead move of all time in any sport. The worst was the Boston Red Sox selling Babe Ruth to the Yankees. Babe Ruth was the best baseball player and the most dynamic and crowd-pleasing guy who ever put on a uniform. Allowing Hull to leave the NHL and the Blackhawks and go to Winnipeg was probably the second-dumbest move after the sale of Ruth.

So here we have a team that used to own the city and then started a long, painful, downhill run that lasted for more than 30 years. I'm not saying that every year was a bad year because the Hawks got to the Stanley Cup Finals against Pittsburgh in the early 1990s, but overall, it was a downhill spiral. You had Wirtz and Bob Pulford keeping their distance from the paying customer, and the team lost a lot of its relevance.

John McDonough is making the right moves as the front man. McDonough is a great public relations man, and he is making all the moves that the team needs to reestablish itself with the public. He's being given the chance to be a good PR man. When Jim DeMaria was in charge of the team's PR, he couldn't make the moves that McDonough has been able to make. DeMaria didn't have those chances because he wasn't allowed to spend the money or put the team on home television.

That's because Rocky Wirtz has completely changed the culture of the team. After his dad died, it was clear Rocky had a plan for this team. They have done so much to get the team back in front of the public eye. Rocky Wirtz obviously knew he wanted to make some moves once he took over the day-to-day operations of the team, and all of those moves are working out beautifully. I think we're seeing that as the Hawks are getting better, the city of Chicago wants to fall in love with this team again. They want the team to have the icons, the stars it used to have. The good will is there—on both sides of the fence. Wirtz, McDonough, and Dale Tallon are making the right moves, and the fans are starting to warm up to the team once again.

The team is getting better. They have the young stars to build off of, and it looks like the supporting cast is getting pretty good, as well. But it's not just a matter of creating good will. At a certain point the team has to win the key games, and they have to win in the playoffs.

That's what it's all about: winning in the postseason. You win a series, and you advance. The more you do that, the better it is for your team and the more fans you will bring back to the sport. They can't expect to do it all at once, but you have to start winning regularly and then winning in the postseason. The PR things that they have done like putting the home games on television and having the Winter Classic at Wrigley Field on New Year's Day, are great things, but ultimately it's about winning.

Can they deliver the Stanley Cup? Here, Patrick Kane (88) celebrates with teammate Jonathan Toews (19) after Toews' goal during the first period of their game against the Phoenix Coyotes in Chicago on Friday, November 30, 2007. (AP Photo/Charles Rex Arbogast)

Michael Jordan learned that with the Bulls. Everyone was calling him the greatest player of all time long before the Bulls won their first title in 1991. It didn't matter to him. He wanted to win a championship. Let's hope Kane and Toews are just as hungry. Let's hope that more than the statistics they put on the board, the goals they score, or the highlight moves they make, they really care about winning and can deliver a championship team to the Chicago sports fans once again. It's been so long since the Blackhawks won the Stanley Cup that it's ridiculous. If those two could ever lead the team to a championship, they would have this city on its knees and the people would be beside themselves with joy. It would be a tremendous thing for the city.

Would it be as big as the Bears winning another Super Bowl, or would it be as big as the Cubs winning the World Series? I'm not going to say that. Nothing would be as big as the Cubs winning the Series. But it would be huge, and I think the city would really embrace it.

I think you would see everyone enjoying it. Most people think African Americans wouldn't be into it, but I don't think that would be the case at all. During the heyday of Hull, Mikita, and those great teams they had in the 1960s, there were always kids around the Stadium playing street hockey, and they weren't just white kids from the suburbs. They were the local kids from the projects, and I think that the whole city would embrace a Hawks championship team.

There's a long way to go, but I like what the team has been doing. They're a lot closer to reaching those goals now than they were two, three, or five years ago. Let's just wait and see how long it takes for them to get there.

Keeping Interest High

The best way to get the fans all the way back is to win a Stanley Cup. I would love to see that, but you can't make it happen right away. Every once in a while, a team that the experts think may not be ready can catch fire and dominate in the postseason. But more often, a team will win a series or two one year and then take the step up the ladder to the championship the following year or maybe two years later.

Along the way, however, you have to play exciting hockey. You need good supporting players to go along with the stars. Kane and Toews are young players with the potential to be superstars, but they are not there yet. What's really encouraging is that they have other players like Kris Versteeg, Patrick Sharp, Duncan Keith, and Brian Campbell who are going to pick up the slack and take some of the heat off the young guys. That's how winning teams do it. They lean on their stars to get the job done, but they have a supporting cast around them so that if the top guys don't have their best games, their teammates will pick up the slack.

While a team is on its way up the ladder, they have to keep things interesting for the fans. You are not going to win every night, but you have to go about your business in an entertaining fashion. That means you have to be willing to drop the gloves and fight once in a while.

Yes, I know it's not politically correct to like fighting in hockey. But you know what? I couldn't care less. I have always wanted to see my team be willing to drop the gloves and fight. Fight for each other and fight to get the crowd into the game. I don't mean a huge brawl involving everybody where both benches empty and everyone is milling around on the ice. Those kinds of things just slow the game down, and that's not really an issue any more. The league has done a good job of getting rid of those kinds of things. Same thing with the stick swinging, I never liked to see that, and it was just a stupid thing for players to do.

But a good one-on-one fight is not a bad thing. For one thing, it brings a team closer together. It shows that teammates are willing to stick up for each other. I think it's the kind of thing that will help in the long run, and it will send a message to the rest of the league. If someone is thinking about taking a run at one of the Blackhawks players, they will have to know that it won't be a free run. You're going to pay a price, and you are going to get challenged by the Blackhawks if you take a cheap shot.

I see quite a few guys on the team who will respond and stand up and fight when challenged. I don't think you should just start something for no reason, but if you see a teammate who is getting punished in the corner or somebody takes a shot at one of your guys, you have to be willing to stand up for them. I think the Blackhawks have guys who will stand up and fight for each other on an every-game basis. Having players like that will only make them develop faster and turn into an excellent team sooner. If you stand up for each other, you get the crowd behind you and the confidence in the locker room grows.

I don't think there's anything wrong with enjoying a good one-on-one fight. If it's clean and there are just two guys who square off and try to get the best of each other, that's fine. I enjoy it, and I think most people who buy tickets like it, as well. If that's barbaric, so be it. If that's politically incorrect, so what? Most people go to the games to see the Blackhawks win, and if you throw in a fight or two, so much the better.

"Most people go to the games to see the Blackhawks win, and if you throw in a fight or two, so much the better."

I'm not apologizing, and I'm sticking to my guns.

6

More Sports Talk

The Yankees

My earliest sports memories as a kid are about baseball—not only the White Sox and the Cubs, but the opponents that came in here and played against us.

When I was a kid, the team I hated the most was the New York Yankees. I don't think that's very unique because a lot of fans in Chicago and around the country hated the Yankees. They were the haves, and we were the have-nots. Back in the late 1950s and early 1960s, we had a lot of good and competitive teams, but not the kind of teams that measured up against the Yankees.

> "When I was a kid, the team I hated the most was the New York Yankees."

Those teams had everything. They would roll into Chicago with Mickey Mantle, Roger Maris, Bobby Richardson, Whitey Ford, and Tony Kubek. Pretty formidable. Who would we trot out to pitch against their lineup? Juan Pizarro. We didn't really have much of a chance to

TOP 5 CHICAGO STEAKHOUSES

1. Wildfire
2. Gibson's Steakhouse
3. Rosewood
4. Gene and Georgetti
5. Tavern on Rush

hang in there with the Yankees over a season because they were just flat-out more talented. Nellie Fox was not about to beat the Yankees all by himself.

And we hated them for it. They had a stranglehold on talent, and in those days there was no free agency. The Yankees could basically hold on to any player they wanted, and it didn't even cost them much. I think Mantle was the only guy who made $100,000 for them, so they were getting all these stars at bargain-basement prices.

When the Yankees finally got old and couldn't replace the talent, they went down and weren't a big factor. But I still hated them, and I was glad to see them lose. Then George Steinbrenner brought the team, and it was obvious he wasn't going to settle for being a loser or being a .500 team. Then the rules changed as free agency gave everyone a chance to go after talented players.

The Yankees, of course, became big-time players in free agency as they signed guys like Reggie Jackson and Catfish Hunter. They were back to being contenders and a strong team. Not the team that won every year like they had in the old days, but they became a team that everybody worried about again.

I guess my feelings have changed over the years. The Yankees weren't in the Sox's division, and I didn't hate them anymore. Most people don't like Steinbrenner—at least most people outside of New

York—but I never felt that way about him. I liked the way he ran his team and felt he was doing everything he could to make his team a winner. I admired the way he ran his team, and I often wanted our teams to be run the same way. Steinbrenner's a guy who will not accept being .500, and he will not accept losing. He did whatever he could to change that and didn't care if he rubbed people the wrong way. He was responsible to himself, his team, and his fans, and he didn't care if some guy in Detroit, Chicago, or Oakland didn't think it was fair. He was telling his competitors that if they didn't like the way he was doing business to go out and get better players and beat him. He was telling the rest of baseball—including the crosstown Mets, the Red Sox, the Cubs, the White Sox, and the Dodgers—to go home and get their shine boxes.

But those old Yankees teams had numerous stars. You couldn't wait to see Mantle, Maris, and Ford come to town to play, and then you couldn't wait to see them leave after they handed out a beating. Mantle had that incredible power, and when he hit a ball it sounded like an explosion.

Buffalo Bills

I've been a Bears fan all my life, but I have to tell you that the most amazing things I've ever seen in football were the four straight Super Bowls the Buffalo Bills went to in the early 1990s.

This team had quite a reputation, and a lot of people put them down because they lost all four of those Super Bowls. But look what they did. They went to four in a row. They had some really good players in Jim Kelly, Andre Reed, and Thurman Thomas along with Bruce Smith, but I'm not sure you would call any of them all-time greats.

I give Marv Levy credit as one of the best coaches in the history of football. How many other coaches took their team to four straight championship games? Not Tom Landry, not Bill Parcells, not Bill Belichick, not Bill Walsh, and not Jimmy Johnson—only Levy.

Other Teams' Stars

Over the years, great players have come to Chicago. In addition to Mantle, when I think of guys who were great hitters, I think of George Brett, Mike Schmidt, Will Clark, Hank Aaron, and Willie Mays.

Brett was a guy who always seemed to kill the White Sox. I remember that left-handed stance of his in Comiskey Park, just ready to launch himself into the ball. Talk about a guy who could hit it all over the ballpark. It seemed like he could drive it anywhere he wanted. If there was a gap in left-center, he would go that way. If there was one in right-center, he'd make some little adjustment with his feet or his hands and drive it there. If he had to pull the ball, it would jump off his bat and fly to the stands. Just an awesome hitter.

Did anybody love hitting in Wrigley Field more than Mike Schmidt? I don't know whether it was the day baseball, the basket in left field, or the Cubs pitching that made him light up when he came to Wrigley Field, but it always seemed that he had two home runs before the fifth inning. If ever there was a hitter who was made to hit at Wrigley Field, it was Schmidt. He would have put together incredible numbers if he had played for the Cubs. But then again, he wouldn't have been hitting off of Cubs pitching.

While the American League had Brett, the National League had Will Clark. Both guys were very similar when they came to the plate. Just very smooth swings and like Brett, Clark could drive it all over the park. He personally knocked the Cubs out of the playoffs in 1989 with his performance in the NLCS. The Cubs couldn't get him out. Clark hit better than .600 against them (13-for-20, .650 batting average, two HRs, eight RBIs), and it seemed like he was up every time the Giants needed a clutch hit. He delivered nearly every time.

Hank Aaron was about as exciting as a glass of warm milk. He was the same every time he came up—expressionless at the plate, focused on his job, and not the least bit excited. But the guy knew what he was doing. Another guy who loved hitting the ball at Wrigley Field, he hit it no matter where the Braves were playing, but there was something about the Cubs pitchers that brought out the best in him.

> Willie Mays was the National League's answer to Mickey Mantle and was simply a great player. As an all-around player nobody ever did it like Mays. Watching him run the bases was unbelievable. He could make any play in the outfield, and he had a great arm. Then there was his aggressiveness at the plate—it seemed like everything he hit was good for extra bases.

As a Bears fan, I have asked myself the question many times: Would it have been better to win Super Bowl XX like the Bears did, or would it have been better to go to four straight Super Bowls?

"I give Marv Levy credit as one of the best coaches in the history of football."

I'm gonna tell you that it is pretty unbelievable for a team to do what the Bills did. To go to four straight Super Bowls is a great accomplishment. Look at the teams they were beating out to get there. They annihilated a great Raiders team to get to their first Super Bowl. The next year, they beat Denver in the AFC Championship Game.

The following year was the 1992 season, and I'm not sure if that wasn't their best accomplishment as far as the postseason is concerned. If you remember, they had a ton of injuries that year and they did not win the AFC East. Instead, they were a Wild Card team. First round, they were at home to Houston and things didn't go their way.

They were down 35–3 in the third quarter, and they didn't even have Kelly. He was hurt. He was out and they went with a backup in Frank Reich. At halftime, everyone was talking about next year and that the Bills were done. Instead, they mounted the greatest comeback in NFL history in any game ever, and they beat the Oilers in overtime. I'll never forget that game, and neither will anyone else. How can you come back from that kind of hole? It's a tribute to Levy and the kind of guys they had on that team.

As if that wasn't enough, they went on the road and beat Pittsburgh the next week and it wasn't even close. They won by three touchdowns. That meant they got to go down to Miami and line up against Dan Marino. You think you are going to beat Miami playing at home in the AFC Championship Game? There's no way, but somebody forgot to tell the Bills.

The Dolphins were strutting all over the place because they beat San Diego 31–0 the week before. But Buffalo rolled them 29–10. They were a completely professional team, and they knew how to play in the postseason. Whether they were at home or on the road, those guys simply went out there and took care of business. The next year they did the same thing beating the Raiders, and then they took care of Joe Montana and the Kansas City Chiefs.

Okay, I know the Bills didn't win any of their Super Bowls, but nobody whipped through all of those playoff games the way the Bills did. Every time out, they were the hunted and they got the job done. If they were favorites, they won the game. If they were underdogs,

TOP 5 HOT DOG/SANDWICH STANDS

1. Roma's (On Cicero)
2. Wolfy's
3. Al's Beef (Northwest Highway, Park Ridge)
4. Gene and Jude's Red Hot Stand
5. Bobo's on Irving Park Road

they figured it out anyway. They're one of the best teams in the history of the NFL, and they don't get the credit.

I give a lot of the credit to Marv Levy. He's a Chicago guy, he's in the Hall of Fame, and he deserves it. Four-year runs like the one they had may come along in baseball, but they don't come along in the NFL. It's one thing to do it when you have a roster filled with Hall of Fame players, but that's not the Bills. They had some players who were awfully good but not all-time greats.

If you put that Bills team in a game against the 1985 Bears, they might have been better prepared than anyone else to give the Bears a good game, but it wouldn't have mattered. The 1985 Bears were too good and would have annihilated them. The Bears were just too strong and explosive.

The Great Steelers Teams

I go with the Steelers when the subject is the greatest football team of all time. The teams they had in the 1970s were so good and so complete that I don't think the other great teams—the 1972–73 Dolphins, the 49ers of the 1980s, the Cowboys of the 1990s, or even the Patriots in this decade—were good enough to beat them on a regular basis.

The Steel Curtain, Mean Joe Greene, Mel Blount, Jack Ham and that whole bunch—everyone knows about their defense and how good and tough they were. They could hit you, and they could knock you out. But the Steelers were no one-dimensional team, and I think that gets lost as time goes by. I'm sure everyone in Pittsburgh knows how good the offense was, but how many people really remember how good a quarterback Terry Bradshaw was when he was leading that team?

Today, people think of Bradshaw as the wise guy on the FOX pregame show, but he was a Hall of Famer with the Steelers and he didn't get in by the skin of his teeth, either. He was a great one who had arm strength and touch. I think that passing game might have given the Steelers the edge on every other great team.

Even the 1985 Bears would have had problems with Bradshaw's Steelers. Would Mike Richardson have been able to cover Lynn Swann? I want to see Leslie Frazier have to battle an outstanding big receiver like John Stallworth. I want to see how that Bears defense would have played against a Steelers team that would not have allowed them to tee off on every play.

That's how the Bears did it. They did it by putting outstanding pressure on the quarterback and punishing the running backs before they had a chance to get to the line of scrimmage. That Steelers team was just too good to let that happen play after play. Their offensive linemen were outstanding, and I don't think anyone has ever seen a better center than Mike Webster. The Steelers offense could beat you with the running game and with the pass.

Franco Harris could take the ball to the outside and get you 20 or 25 yards a crack. Rocky Bleier wasn't fancy, but when he went inside, he would get a short-yardage first down or even break a big play. When you can run the ball the way that they did, and when you have the kind of passing game that can hit the medium-range passes and the deep passes, that would have given the Bears some trouble.

I'm not saying the Bears defense wouldn't have gotten to Bradshaw because they would have. It would have been like a heavyweight fight between two great champions. Each side would have given as good as they got, and it would have been a hell of a battle.

The Steelers offense was really overlooked. Everyone talks about how good the Steel Curtain defense was, and it was one of the most gifted defenses to ever play the game. But they owe a big debt to the Steelers offense because they were great when it came to winning the time-of-possession battle every week. The Steelers defense didn't have to stay on the field 35 or 40 minutes a game because the Steelers offense did its part.

"Each side would have given as good as they got, and it would have been a hell of a battle."

The Steelers could hit you with the big plays when they needed to, but they could also grind it out. Their first two championship teams were more running oriented, and the last two Super Bowl teams (of the 1970s) were more passing oriented, but both teams were balanced. The running team could pass it when they needed to, and the passing team could run it when they wanted to. They were rarely a burden to the Steelers defense. Sure, there were some low-scoring games in there where the defense dominated, but more often than not, the offense did its share. And sometimes that share was very impressive with big plays from Bradshaw to Stallworth and Swann.

So this was truly a great team, the team that I think was the best of all time or at least the last 50 years. I love Lambert, Ham, and Andy Russell, but I think that the defense may be just a tad overrated because the offense is so underrated. They had stars at every position on offense and could beat you any way you wanted to play. Okay, check that—maybe the tight ends were just ordinary. But Harris and Bleier were stars at the running back position, Bradshaw was a great Hall of Famer at quarterback, and it's hard to top Swann and Stallworth as a quality pair of wide receivers. You can put others in the same team picture with them, but to find a better pair than those two, I don't think so.

So getting back to the picture of Richardson trying to cover Swann and Frazier trying to stay with Stallworth, it would have been tough for the Bears. If the Steelers offensive line could have withstood the pressure of the Bears pass rush, I have to think Swann and Stallworth would have won their battles. Not that they would have killed them, but they would have been good enough to give the Steelers the edge over the long haul.

Now if the Bears pressure up front could get to Bradshaw regularly, it would be a different story. But as good as the Bears were with Otis Wilson, Wilber Marshall, Richard Dent, Dan Hampton, Steve McMichael, and Mike Singletary, I just don't think they could have dominated that great Steelers offensive front.

The Steelers would have known how to adjust to the speed and power of that pass rush. Just like Dan Marino did in the Monday night football game in1985, there would have been a lot of rollouts and quick passes. The Steelers were so good and so experienced that they would have made it awfully tough for the Bears to punish them the way they did so many other teams. This was not the 1985 New England Patriots we're talking about. This is the 1970s Pittsburgh Steelers. They were the best team to ever play, and they would not have been intimidated by the great 1985 Bears.

Wilt Chamberlain

Nearly everybody will tell you that Michael Jordan was the greatest basketball player of all time.

Except me.

Don't get me wrong. I love Jordan, and he was responsible for the six championships the Bulls won. He could do it all, and he had unbelievable will when he was on the court. He hated losing, and when he decided he needed to work on some part of his game, like outside shooting, he did it and became a great outside shooter.

I love Jordan, and maybe I should have treated him better on the air. We'll get into that again later.

But as good as Jordan was, he was not as good as Wilt Chamberlain. Chamberlain was the greatest basketball player ever and one of the greatest athletes of all time. He was the dominant player at a time when there were so many great centers in the game. That's not the case anymore.

The Chairman of the Board—Frank Sinatra

I have talked about Frank for years, and a lot of people wonder why I have such an interest in him. Well, for one thing, he's Frank Sinatra, and that's a good enough reason right there. Another is that when I was a kid growing up, my mom often had his music playing in the house. She was a fan, and so it was a part of what we heard while we were growing up.

I actually got to meet Frank when I was in Vegas years ago. It was 1992 or '93 at the very beginning of the Score and we were in Vegas. We were staying at the famous Desert Inn—a place that no longer exists, but it had been extremely popular. If you were going to Vegas, you wanted to stay at the DI. It was Frank's place, and a lot of the Rat Pack would go there and so would a lot of people from Chicago.

Personally, I had been more of a Dean Martin guy. I just liked his routine. He was this easygoing guy, always had a drink in his hand. He was about the most laid-back guy ever. But Sinatra was always on in the house when I was growing up, so there was this natural appeal. And besides that, he was Sinatra.

I had friends in Vegas and my friends had friends, and one time when we were staying at the DI, I got a chance to meet "Tony O," who was Sinatra's manager. By the end of the conversation, Tony asked me if Be-Be and I would like to see Sinatra perform that night. Of course we said yes.

We got to sit right in the front row, and I was later told it was Frank's booth. They sent over a bottle of champagne. As the show was going on, Sinatra looked at us and gave us the thumbs up. It was a pretty big thrill.

And then we got the invite from Tony. "Mr. Sinatra would like you to join him in the Forum Lounge after the show."

Well, we were stunned. To have the chance to sit in his booth is one thing, but to be invited to his personal party was another. We went into the room after the show and there were maybe 30 people there, some of whom I recognized as being from Chicago and some of whom I didn't. Me and Be-Be were sitting there, but not really even drinking. Instead, we were just sitting back and taking it all in. Keely Smith, a contemporary of Sinatra's who used to collaborate with him from time to time, was singing in the room. Finally, Sinatra came in and he chatted with us and then moved on to talk with a few of his people.

After a while, Frank was still sitting and talking and I thought that was basically all that was gonna happen. I turned to Be and we started to get up, and as we made our way to the door, I heard a voice that made the hair on the back of my neck stand up, "Where do you think you're going?" Frank asked. I was pretty shocked, but I just turned around and told him I was going to the bathroom.

He said I better come back because he wanted to talk to me. So I came back and he started talking to me. "So what do you do?"

"I'm a talk-show host in Chicago," I told him.

Sinatra took that to mean I was some kind of DJ and started talking about music, taking the tone that the music of the time didn't compare with the music of Dean Martin, Elvis Presley, or Cole Porter. "They don't write good music anymore," he said.

So I decided to get into it with him. "Well, what about the Beatles? You've covered their songs before," I said. Sinatra did a version of "Something" which was written by George Harrison. He called it the best Beatles song ever written.

 "Sinatra did a version of 'Something' which was written by George Harrison. He called it the best Beatles song ever written."

He looked at me with an amused look and said that song was written in the 1960s. "That was a long time ago," Sinatra said. "I stand by my statement. They don't write good songs anymore."

And then I decided to set the record straight. "Mr. Sinatra," I told him, "I'm not a disc jockey. I'm a sports talk show host."

He didn't miss a beat and he turned the conversation to sports. The topic: his favorite team, the Los Angeles Dodgers. He went on about the team and Tommy Lasorda and we kicked the subject around for quite a while. It was obvious that he loved baseball and the Dodgers.

We talked for a few minutes and I got to tell him who I was and what I did before I got the radio show. He said "God bless you" and he took the pack of Camels and put them in my pocket and told me he enjoyed meeting me.

The Camels were still wrapped with the plastic around them. I guess that was his way of acknowledging me and giving me something to show that we had sat down and had a conversation. I thanked him, shook his hand, and left.

What I should have done was hand the pack of Camels back to him and ask him to autograph them. I pretty much say what's on my mind and do what I think is the right thing without any hesitation. This is one time I didn't. I would have liked to have that autograph, but I just didn't ask. I don't know why, but I couldn't push it that far.

It wasn't long after that that Sinatra started to lose his faculties and would struggle to complete songs even though he had sung those songs for decades and had the words right in front of him. He passed away in 1998.

Meeting him was a huge thrill and a memory I'll have forever.

Where are the great centers? You have Shaq and you have Tim Duncan, but where are the rest? And Duncan's more like a combination forward-center anyway.

But when Chamberlain was playing, he had to go up against Bill Russell, Nate Thurmond, Willis Reed, Wes Unseld, and guys like that who were talented and big and strong. Everybody tries to say that Russell was better than Chamberlain because of all the championships the Celtics won when he was there, but that really has nothing to do with the truth. The Celtics won championships because Russell was a great player who was surrounded by a great team. He didn't do it alone. He had John Havlicek, Bob Cousy, Sam Jones, and Don Nelson. He wasn't anywhere close to Chamberlain as an offensive player. And Wilt may have been his equal—or at least close to it—on the defensive end. It's not a fair comparison.

Wilt did it all on the court, and he was a spectacular athlete. He ran track and field as a kid from Philadelphia, he was probably the best volleyball player who ever lived, and he could have done anything he wanted. If he had wanted to play in the NFL, I'll bet he could have done that. He almost got into the ring with Muhammad Ali, for crying out loud. Can you imagine anyone doing that today? There was never anyone like that.

 "Chamberlain was the greatest basketball player ever and one of the greatest athletes of all time."

But besides everything he did on the court, he was a great gentleman. I'm not talking about what he said in his book about taking 20,000 ladies to bed—I mean when he came to Chicago and he came on my TV show and went out to dinner with me and my wife and the producers from the show.

Wilt was nothing but a regular guy when he was with me. We went out to dinner at Fairbanks Restaurant. It's in the Hollywood Casino in Aurora where we were doing the TV show. Wilt made plenty of his own comments about his sexual appetites, but let me tell you, he could really put away the food. After the show, he ate two 4-pound lobsters, a huge steak, salad, two bottles of Dom Perignon, and dessert. He called that feast, "a nice little meal to get me through the rest of the day."

It was amazing to watch him put that food away and do it so quickly. He drank the Dom like it was soda pop. I never saw anything like it.

But I was so impressed because he was such a nice guy and such a gentleman. He couldn't have been nicer to Be, and he was great to have as a guest on the show.

Wilt Chamberlain was the greatest basketball player ever to set foot on the court. Here he puts up a short jump shot during a playoff game against the Bucks in Milwaukee, Wisconsin, on April 16, 1972. The Bucks Kareem Abdul-Jabbar was unable to stop the score. (AP Photo)

He was not a modest guy, either. He was more than willing to talk about Bill Russell and Michael Jordan, and he said he was clearly better than either one of them. There was no jealousy in his voice, he was simply stating his opinion as if it was fact. He didn't convince me because I didn't need convincing. I always believed that Chamberlain had the best all-around game of anyone who had ever taken the court. If I wasn't going to change my mind when Jordan was on the top of his game, I don't think I'm going to change my mind with anybody else.

Here's something a lot of people don't realize. While Chamberlain and Russell went after each other on the court and are generally looked at as the top two centers the game has ever seen, the two were anything but rivals off the court. They had a genuine friendship that went both ways. Russell would often stay at Chamberlain's house when the Celtics were playing in Philadelphia or Los Angeles, and they got along great. They often shared Thanksgiving dinner together if the two teams were in close proximity on Thanksgiving Day.

It wasn't a matter of two top-of-the-line athletes just continuing their competition in the off-hours. Instead, they talked about things that were happening in the world, music, social movements, and personalities. Chamberlain said that he and Russell would have been friends even if there had been no basketball. That's how much the two had in common and how much they liked each other.

Pete Rose

I was always a big supporter of Pete Rose. He said he never bet on baseball, and he held that position for years and years. Then when he decided to write his book and there was this feeling in the air that he just might get reinstated by the powers that be, he gave a half-hearted admission that yes, he did bet on baseball.

I didn't like that. He had sat right on the set of my TV show and looked me in the eye and told me he had never bet on baseball. He had done that with a lot of people. To come out so many years later and admit he was lying, what did that really do? Do you think people are going to believe you all of a sudden? You carry a lie like that around, and that's what people will know you for—lying.

But when he came on my television show, he had been a man of honor. My producer Jesse Rogers had booked him to come on the show in the fall of 1999. And at that time, Rose had just been named to the All-Century baseball team. Major League Baseball made a big show out of the entire thing because they introduced the team at the World Series that year, and they had brought in many of the living players to the World Series in Atlanta (against the New York Yankees) and introduced them during the pregame show. Rose was one of them, and this was the first and only time that he had been invited back to a major league ballpark since his gambling troubles had come to light. The league made a decision that since he was a part of this group of great players, he deserved the opportunity to show up and be a part of the festivities.

Rose was introduced, and he got a big ovation from the crowd in Atlanta. Naturally, he was going to be interviewed. I guess he was under the impression that the questions would have to do with being part of the All-Century team, the great players he had played with and against, and the World Series between the Yankees and the Braves. But, of course, it wasn't anything like that. Rose was interviewed by Jim Gray who got right onto the betting on baseball allegations. I guess he surprised Rose because Pete said he didn't want to talk about it and that the ceremony was supposed to be a baseball celebration. But of course, Gray was all over him and wouldn't let anything go. He kept asking him and asking him about betting on baseball and Rose held his ground until the interview ended.

That was the only time I think Pete had gained any sympathy in this whole gambling thing. Gray came off like such a jerk that people felt a little bit sorry for Rose. I thought this was great because we had him scheduled to come on the next show. And then Jesse got a call from Pete, saying with all the fallout from the Gray interview that he was going to back out.

As far as I was concerned, that was an absolute disaster. We had sold out the restaurant at Basta Pasta, and this was going to be a huge thing. This was going to be Rose's first public appearance since the Gray interview, and not only were we getting calls from people to see if they could get in, we were getting calls from other media outlets who wanted to get in so they could make it a big story in their newspaper or magazine or TV broadcast. This was going to be absolutely huge.

So there was no way I could allow him to just back out. I called Pete and kept calling him until he finally picked up the phone. "I understand how you're feeling, but you can't back out on us," I said. "Nobody believes you more than I do, and nobody has backed you more than I have. But if you back out on us now, you will be dead to me."

Maybe I was a little too dramatic and over the top, but that was how I felt. We simply had too much riding on this thing to just let him go and make it easy for him to forget about his commitment.

"Maybe I was a little too dramatic and over the top, but that was how I felt."

Well, it worked out. Pete showed up, and we had a great show. Not only was it a complete sellout, but Chicago camera crews from Channels 2, 5, 7, and 9 showed up, and shows like *Access Hollywood* and *Extra* were there and they all wanted every word that was said. Of course, we talked about the gambling thing because we had to. Pete was denying everything and said he would swear on a stack of Bibles that he didn't bet on baseball. That was his line at the time, and he said it to me and to others.

But then we got into talking about his career and what had motivated him while he was on the baseball field. He said that every time he took the field, he took it personally and that he wanted to be the best guy out there and give his team a chance to win. I never heard anybody more convincing when talking about being a competitor and wanting to win so much—unless we're talking about Michael Jordan. I guess he had as much or more than Pete did when it comes to competitiveness. But look at everything this guy did on the baseball field. He was an All-Star at five different positions, and he never complained about going from second base to third base to left field to right field to first base. He just did what he had to do to help his team win. All the while, he was this feared hitter who would find a way to come through in clutch situations. You can't ask for more fire than that from any ballplayer. You want fire on the field, Pete Rose had it.

I think the play that best shows what Pete Rose was all about was when he crashed into Ray Fosse in the All-Star Game. They break that play out around the All-Star Game every year, and I don't know that people really understand how important the All-Star Game was to Rose and how much he wanted to win.

They had to give home-field advantage in the World Series to the winner of the All-Star Game to at least make it somewhat important again, but back in the day, it was never like that. Rose wanted to beat those American Leaguers, and he would do everything in his power to do it. People say that nobody today would ever go crashing into a catcher the way Rose did to Fosse. Well, you know what? Nobody else but Rose would have done it back then. That's how much of a competitor he was. He wanted it bad, and he basically ruined Fosse's career. He dislocated his shoulder, and while Fosse did come back and had half-decent numbers, he was on his way to becoming a star until Rose ran into him.

I think what makes the story even more amazing is that Rose and Fosse were friends. They had dinner together the night before, and Rose really liked him. Then he ran over him like that just to win an All-Star Game. You can't ask for more fire than Pete Rose showed on that play or in his whole career.

Pete Rose the ballplayer is one thing, but Pete Rose the man is something else. The bottom line is that he lied to me and to everybody else. When he came out in his own book and admitted that he bet on baseball, it just smelled bad. He was trying to sell books and pave his way into the Hall of Fame. That part has not worked out so well for him. He may have eventually told the truth, but he did it for all the wrong reasons.

I think that has left an even more bitter taste than it would have if Pete had just held on to his original story. You can't lie like that for years and finally tell the truth for very questionable reasons and think it will clear your name. It has not for Rose.

I had Pete Rose on my radio show as well as my TV show several times. He was not going to admit to anything in terms of betting on baseball…or anything else for that matter. Pete was always hustling throughout his career, and he played nearly every day. He was not the type to take a day off. I asked him if he had ever taken "greenies," which have been banned by baseball in the last couple of years but were always available back in the day. (The pills taken were amphetamines, and "greenies" was the common nickname for them.) It wasn't something that was outside of baseball's rules.

Pete never admitted to taking greenies. The only thing he said was that he would often report to spring training a few pounds overweight—maybe five or six—and that in order to get in tip-top shape, he would take diet pills during spring training. But as far as taking greenies on a regular basis, he denied it.

But someone who lived so hard during his playing career—both on the field and off—you really have to wonder if he did or not. I asked him about the times he would come to Chicago with the Reds for a three- or four-game weekend series and play nothing but day games, leaving plenty of opportunities for fun in the after hours.

"I had my fun," Rose said. "I was no goodie-goodie. But there was a difference between me and a lot of the other players. I did take care of my body. I may have stayed up or gone out, but I never drank and I never smoked. That was not the case with a lot of other guys. I'm not saying I didn't chase a little bit, but I didn't have to stay out to all hours to take care of what I wanted. I still took somebody home with me. But I did not have to wait until 2:00 or 3:00 in the morning. You can go out and enjoy the night life and still get your rest and play your best game the next day. If we had gone out all night on Thursday night and all night on Friday night, there's no way we could have played on Saturday. We knew what our priorities were, and we took care of them."

One thing I can say about Pete is that he has never wanted to see others suffer just because he has been punished. He could easily have gone after Barry Bonds and called him a cheating son of a bitch—which he is—but he didn't. Bond's head grew two hat sizes. Baseball didn't make steroids illegal until the 2004 season, and Pete always said that he didn't care who did them and who didn't until baseball banned them. "If somebody did steroids after the ban went into affect and baseball can prove it, then you punish them and start taking things away," Rose said. "But if it happened before or it hasn't been proven, then I don't care. I broke the rules, and I've been suspended ever since. There were no rules on steroids before 2004.

"Baseball dropped the ball on steroids in 1998 and 1999. They wanted to bring the fans back with the home run. They have all these small ballparks and you have a lively ball and when you have short-stops hitting home runs to the opposite field and Brady Anderson hitting 50 home runs one year and 18 the next, it's obvious they got what they wanted. The home run brought people back and got everybody talking about baseball again."

7

Good Trade, Bad Trade

GOING OUT AND GETTING CARLOS QUENTIN could turn out to be the best move Kenny Williams has made as general manager of the White Sox.

Nothing is guaranteed, but Quentin looks like he is going to be a consistent hitter with plenty of power for years to come. He is strong, he has a good eye, and he is obviously very hungry. I like his stroke, and I like the way he plays defense.

Breaking his wrist in a fit of anger after fouling off a pitch against the Indians was not a good thing, and it certainly hurt him and the team in

After breaking his wrist on Monday, September 1, 2008, all Carlos could do was watch the team from the dugout. (AP Photo)

2008, but I don't think he's going to do that again. I think he'll learn from his mistakes, and that's what you want to see from a young player.

The other thing that injury told you is that Quentin is an emotional and passionate guy who really cares about his job. I think he has a chance to be a guy who hits 30 homers, drives in 100 runs, and hits about .300 for years to come. If he can do that—or even come close to it—this will be considered one of the great trades in team history.

The White Sox gave the Arizona Diamondbacks first baseman Chris Carter for Quentin. At the time Williams made the trade, it was not a big deal. Quentin had injuries, and a lot of people no longer considered him to be the top prospect he once was. But Williams is a guy who will stick by his guns. Sometimes that's going to help him and other times that's going to hurt him. In this case, it will help him.

You really have to applaud Williams in this case because Quentin's numbers were not very impressive when he was given a chance to play in the majors prior to the trade. He had a lifetime average of .230 with 14 homers and 63 RBI in 138 major-league games. Numbers like that are ordinary, and Williams could have easily turned his back and gone after somebody else. But Kenny wasn't just looking at the numbers—he was looking at the player, his swing, his strengths, his weaknesses, and came to the conclusion that Quentin could be a guy that sits in the middle of the lineup and produces for years to come. That's what a good general manager does. He has to make decisions based on the numbers and also based on his instincts. If he thinks a player is the real deal even though the numbers aren't great, a good general manager will take his shot and make sure that the player gets an opportunity to prove himself.

I think the Quentin deal is going to be one of the best trades in White Sox history.

But as a Chicago guy, it's not the good deals that we want to talk about. It's the bad ones. And there's one that stands out to me even though it's been more than 40 years. The Chicago Blackhawks had a good team in the 1960s, and they had a chance to be great. Then they traded Phil Esposito to the Boston Bruins, and by doing so they hurt themselves and gave the Bruins a huge boost that would help them win a couple of Stanley Cups.

"I think the Quentin deal is going to be one of the best trades in White Sox history."

Here was the deal. I know a lot of Blackhawks fans may not want to read about it even now because it's just too painful. The Hawks traded Esposito, Ken Hodge, and Fred Stanfield to the Bruins for Pit Martin, Gilles Marotte, and Jack Norris.

Let's look at the other guys before we get into Espo. Hodge was a big right winger who turned out to be a 50-goal scorer and was a very good if not great player in his own right. He may not have been the fastest skater, but he could shoot and score. Stanfield was a good player who was pretty versatile. I know he played center and also played the point on the power play.

Now look at who the Hawks got. Okay, Martin was a pretty good player who had a good shot and could put the puck in the net. Was he a dominant guy or anything close to that? No way in the world. He was a good player, and that's it. Marotte was a stay-at-home defenseman who could throw a body check. Norris? The guy was a backup goalie for crying out loud. He gave the Hawks nothing.

So even without Espo, this trade was a win for the Bruins and a loss for the Hawks. With Espo, it was one of the worst of all time. He would go on to score 40 or more goals in seven straight years, 50 or more five times, and he had 76 goals and 76 assists in his best year 1970–71.

When the Blackhawks made the trade, head coach Billy Reay wasn't sure about Esposito. He thought he might turn out to be a decent player, but he never thought he would be a dominant scorer.

Well, Reay missed on that one. I remember the Bruins were so popular in Boston at the time that there was a bumper sticker that really showed how popular and loved that team was. The bumper sticker read, "Jesus Saves…and Espo scores on the rebound." Funny, clever, and to the point. It was all good times in Boston, and we could have had those good times here in Chicago. It was a terrible trade that set this franchise back a long way.

What makes it hurt so much more is that when the two teams met in the playoffs, Phil Esposito scored like crazy against his brother Tony, and the Bruins won the series. If Phil was here along with Ken Hodge and they had Martin and Marotte, I think we would have had a better chance of winning—even if the Bruins did have Bobby Orr. We had no chance because that trade was so lopsided.

Old-time Blackhawks fans still feel the pain from that one.

8

Announcers

THEY ARE IN OUR LIVING ROOMS AND IN OUR CARS. They are our link to the team. No matter how many games you go to, nobody can get to all of them, so in order to fully get the feel of your team, you have to listen to your team's play-by-play announcers and take what they say to heart. In many cases, you hear from them more than members of your own family—and for a lot of people, they are family.

Here are my favorite play-by-play announcers that I have heard here in Chicago.

Jack Brickhouse

You can't just list Jack as the voice of the Cubs. He was the voice of the Cubs, White Sox, and the Bears, and he was great no matter which team he was covering. He did it all, and he was the guy everybody knew. He was in our cars, our living rooms, and our bedrooms, for crying out loud. Brickhouse was as good as any of the national announcers, only he was all ours. I know he did a few national events, but he was doing the Cubs and the White Sox and the Bears and he was a Chicago guy. He even did pro wrestling.

One of the things I liked best about him was that you couldn't tell if the Cubs were winning or losing. His tone of the voice was always interested and excited by what he was seeing. He didn't cry if they were

One of Chicago's greatest announcers was the late Jack Brickhouse who called games for the Cubs, White Sox, and Bears. (AP Photo)

losing, and he wouldn't go overboard if they were winning. He was the same and had an even-keel tone to his voice. His homerun call was a classic. "Hey Hey" was his signature, and at the time it hit the nail right on the head—it was everything a baseball fan needed to hear.

"Brickhouse was as good as any of the national announcers, only he was all ours."

Here's another thing that I loved about Jack that almost never gets discussed: he had great interviewing skills. He knew how to get great answers out of athletes, coaches, or anyone else he talked to. He knew how to draw people out, and he would vary his technique with each person. Obviously, if somebody was very talkative, it would be an easy interview for him and he wouldn't have to say a lot. But if somebody was on the quiet side, he did a great job of making him feel comfortable so he would talk and open up. I don't think Jack just wanted some guest to come on the air and babble. He would bring out real information, something the listener on the other end of the television or radio wanted to hear. I remember him doing that with Stan Musial when I was a kid. Stan was a nice guy and obviously one of the best hitters of his era. But he was not that forthcoming with his words or information. However, when he was on the air with Jack, he would open up and say plenty.

So Jack was a very versatile broadcaster who would be on the air almost every day—at least that's how it seemed. He was doing baseball in the summer and football in the fall, and he was great. He was the king of Chicago's announcers for a very long time, and he was just a great listen.

Lloyd Pettit

I don't think there's a more difficult sport to announce than ice hockey. In baseball you have a starting lineup, and the game moves at an easy pace until the late innings. Once you get into it, there really aren't a lot of things that the announcer has to worry about.

Now take a look at ice hockey. After you start the game with your five skaters and a goalie, a new line and a new defense pairing jumps out there after a minute or a minute and a half, and that's the way the game rolls. You have to stay on top of all the line changes for a 60-minute game and describe action that is moving so quickly. The game requires a lot of description, so you have to speak quickly, know what you have to talk about, and know what you have to let go if you are going to give the audience the complete story.

Nobody did that better than Lloyd Pettit. He was a very thorough and complete announcer and his signature, "A shot and a goal," is a real classic. Much different than the "He shoots, he scores," that so many announcers use today. I'm not saying that's a bad way to go, either. It's just that Lloyd's call was so sharp and unique. He was different than everybody else, and he was clearly an original.

Pettit's description of the game was so clear. Hockey's a tough sport to broadcast, but it's also a tough sport to listen to since so much is going on and announcers have to work fast. But when Pettit was doing the game, you could almost see the action as the words came out of his mouth. You could see Bobby Hull streaking down the left side as he spoke those words. You could see Stan Mikita's pass land right on the stick of Dennis Hull. You could see Chico Maki face off against Pete Stemkowski. That's what made him a magical announcer—he took the most difficult game in the world to announce and he made his listeners feel as if they were part of it. That's what made him great.

One other thing on Pettit: he was incredible when it came to announcing hockey fights. He knew exactly what he was doing. Pettit would describe Keith Magnuson throwing "a left, a left, another left, and a straight right." Well, I guess Maggie was usually on the receiving end instead of throwing most of those punches. But the point is that when the fights happened, Pettit didn't shy away and act like he was embarrassed because there was fighting in the sport. I think he enjoyed doing the blow-by-blow, and I know that those of us who were listening really got a kick out of it.

"…he was incredible when it came to announcing hockey fights."

He was the best hockey announcer I ever heard, and I know Pat Foley patterned himself after Pettit. Foley does a great job as well, but as far as I'm concerned, nobody will ever top the original.

Jack Quinlan

A lot of people might not remember Jack Quinlan, but those of us who heard him knew he was a great announcer. He had a great voice, and he was the first announcer I ever heard doing the Cubs games.

For those of you who don't know him, Jack started doing the Cubs games in 1956 and he did them through the 1964 season. He was with the Cubs at spring training in 1965, and he was killed in a car accident as he returned from a charity golf outing.

What a great loss that was. He was a very skilled announcer and a really easy listen. Like all the greats, when you were listening to Quinlan you felt like you were right there and part of the event. It was a tragic passing because he was such a young guy (38 years old) and he clearly had a great future.

Harry Caray

Where do you start with Harry? He was this amazing whirlwind of a guy who started over when he came to Chicago and was paired with Jimmy Piersall to call White Sox games. He had done the Cardinals games in St. Louis for such a long time that he was closely identified with them. Then he went to Oakland for a year, and it was not a good fit. Then he came to Chicago and if you look at it closely, it could have been a desperate situation.

But instead of starting to bounce from job to job, Harry established a unique Chicago identity. Here's why he made it so big here—he was just like you and me. Despite being the White Sox announcer and then going on to even greater heights with the Cubs, he never thought he was anything more than just a lucky baseball fan who got the chance to broadcast games.

I remember one summer a bunch of us were on the way to vend at Comiskey Park when we spotted Harry coming out of a dry cleaner's just a block or two from where he used to live at the Ambassador

Harry Caray, then a radio announcer for the Chicago White Sox, bellows his emphatic, "Holy Cow" during a game against the Baltimore Orioles in Chicago on July 5, 1972. (AP Photo/les)

East Hotel. We yelled, "Hey Harry," and he came right over and started talking with us about baseball and just about anything else. It was easy. We were just young guys who were trying to make a living, and Harry was more than happy to take time out and talk to us. That's what made him so successful. He had no airs about him, and he was friendly.

Now that's not to say that Harry couldn't be a red ass if he wanted to. If somebody got under his skin, he would let you know about it. But he was this guy who loved what he was doing, and he always identified with the people, and that's what made him so successful. People know when somebody is legitimate and being themselves, and they know when somebody is trying to snow them. Harry was the last guy in the world who would try to fool people and be a phony.

He was legitimate and just the kind of guy who was fun to talk to, fun to listen to, and fun to hear calling a game.

> "Harry was the last guy in the world who would try to fool people and be a phony."

You had to respect him because of where he came from. He was a guy who made it on his own. He didn't have anyone clearing the way for him and setting him up with a broadcast job. He had to do it himself, and he was not afraid to stand up for himself and break down a few doors. He was forward, pushy, and he did what he needed to in order to get a job that so many people wanted. You had to respect that.

Did he butcher names? Of course he did. But I think that was a big part of the Harry charm, and it's one of the reasons his name lives on all these years after his death. His trademark phrases of "Holy Cow" and "It might be, it could be, it is…a home run" will live on forever.

Jim Durham

He was simply as smooth as he could be in all the years he broadcast Bulls games. A lot of past and present announcers always injected themselves into the broadcast and tried to make it all about them. That was not Durham, who was really crisp in his descriptions of the Bulls.

Now, I'm not saying he was the best businessman in the world or had the best agent. He tried to negotiate a new deal after the Bulls won their first championship, and I guess he didn't read the situation very well. He was a good broadcaster for them—actually, he was an excellent broadcaster for them. But it's not like he couldn't be replaced. That's what he found out first hand, and he didn't get to broadcast the Bulls great championship run. That was too bad for him.

I really liked listening to him describe the action and do it in such a smooth fashion. He has done well since leaving the Bulls, and he has handled quite a few national broadcasts. He's good at that, but not quite as good as when he was doing the local broadcasts of the Bulls. That was his best work, and he was really in his heyday early in the Michael Jordan era. He knew how great Michael was, but he never oversold it or undersold it. He had just the right touch for the Bulls.

9

Biggest Busts

CHICAGO SPORTS FANS HAVE HAD MORE THAN OUR SHARE of bums, villains, busts, and failures. Guys like Cade McNown, Curtis Enis, Juan Pierre, Dave Smith, Candy Maldonado, and Nick Swisher have really stunk it up around here and have made fans angry and disappointed with the way they have worn Chicago uniforms. There are dozens more as well, but here are the three Chicago athletes who I think have been the worst players to ever wear Chicago uniforms.

Cedric Benson, Bears

This guy was awful from the start for the Bears, and I don't think there's anything but embarrassment coming from Jerry Angelo when the Bears made this pick in 2005. Benson was supposed to be a stud of a running back when the Bears drafted him from Texas, but you could tell he was soft from the minute they drafted him. There he was, one of the top picks overall in the draft, and the first time he's talking to reporters, he's complaining about the "process" and how he didn't like being under the microscope.

Oh, poor Cedric. What in the world was he thinking? That they were going to change the system just for him? That's ridiculous. You want your first-round draft pick to come in and say that he wants to get out on the football field and kick some ass. There was none of

Bears running back Cedric Benson runs with the ball during the third quarter of an NFL game against the Minnesota Vikings on Sunday, December 3, 2006, in Chicago. Unfortunately, Benson wasn't the back the Bears hoped he would be. (AP Photo)

that fire with Cedric Benson. If you don't have it as a rookie running back, when are you going to get it? Your second year? Your fourth year? No, you're not going to get it at all. No fire. No competitiveness. It's called weak stock.

Benson was awful in his rookie year and he did somewhat better in 2006, the year the Bears went to the Super Bowl. Benson alternated with Thomas Jones and he played decently, so the team traded Thomas Jones. Give me a break. Jones came into his own with the Bears and gave them the kind of running game that Benson was never going to give them.

So why did the Bears fall apart in 2007? One of the reasons was that they had no running game. Benson didn't have the fight, the willpower, or the desire to get out on the field and produce. He was a disappointment, and at least the Bears had the decency to draft Matt Forte in 2008, give him the starting running back position, and get rid of Benson. There he was getting drunk on his boat during the off-season and the team didn't need him.

It was a long time before anyone picked up Benson, and it's no surprise that Cincinnati was the team that picked him up. They have had nothing but personnel issues, so he fits their system. And then what does he do when he gets to the Bengals? He mouths off. He starts talking about Forte and saying that Forte did a good job but that if he was still in Chicago, he would have had a better year. Okay. Go ahead. Keep talking and continue to make an ass of yourself. Nobody believes that garbage anyway.

Eddie Robinson, Chicago Bulls

This guy set the record for most money and least productivity. The Bulls gave this guy $32 million for absolutely nothing. All he did was sit in the trainer's room with his injuries, and he never gave the Bulls anything for their money. He was content to sit on the bench with a towel on his lap while resting comfortably. Did he want to play? Was he going to contribute anything as a shooter? Was he going to make the team better in any way? Not a prayer. Robinson never seemed the least bit interested in anything except cashing his check.

This was a huge mistake by Jerry Krause, and it's one of the reasons he was never able to make any progress after Michael Jordan left and the great Bulls team crumbled. Krause had a hard time relating to most players, and he couldn't bring in too many good players. And then when he made a signing, it was for this guy who never gave the Bulls anything. It was bad for the team, and it was bad for the fans who packed the United Center every night to watch him sit.

Todd Hundley, Chicago Cubs

Hundley was supposed to be a fan favorite when he signed with the Cubs because his dad, Randy Hundley, had been such a solid player for the Cubs in the 1960s and '70s. While Randy was a great guy and a hard worker, Todd never came across that way, and his performance on the field was just abominable more often than not. He couldn't hit once he got to the Cubs. He had some big years with the Mets and had hit quite a few home runs, but clutch hits with the Cubs were few and far between. He didn't exactly respond to criticism very well, either, and he made it difficult for fans to have faith that he would ever turn things around and become a productive player. There was also quite a bit of immaturity as he gave the finger to a fan after hitting one of his rare home runs. So he did nothing but disappoint people on the field, and he didn't act very well off of it.

10

Best Chicago Sports Venues

I'VE SAID THIS BEFORE AND I WILL SAY IT AGAIN: one of the most important reasons Chicago is the No. 1 sports city in this country is that all of the teams based here play in the city itself. In New York, the Giants and Jets both do their business in New Jersey. Not that there's anything wrong with Jersey—my guy Frank Sinatra comes from Jersey—but how can they call themselves the New York Football Giants when they play across the river in New Jersey?

Boston has built a pretty good football team with the Patriots. Those guys play in Foxboro. That's about 45 minutes from Boston. I can't say they don't have the correct name because they are in Massachusetts, so the New England title fits, but you mean to tell me that it wouldn't mean more to the city if the Patriots were in Boston?

I guess Philadelphia meets all the criteria since the Phillies, Eagles, 76ers, and Flyers all play in the city. Good for them. You'll notice I mentioned the Phillies. They have one baseball team, and we have two. They had two, and the A's moved away. So Philadelphia couldn't possibly qualify as a better sports town than Chicago.

That's the major competition. Bring up any other city—St. Louis, Pittsburgh, Denver—we have them beat any way you want to look at it. Those cities don't have the sports history that Chicago does or match up in any other way.

Now that we've got that settled, I want to take a look at the places that make Chicago special as a sports town. I want to look at the best sports venues in the city—the places that have had the best atmosphere for a fan to go and watch a game. I'm talking about the places from the past as well as the current stadiums that call Chicago home.

1. Wrigley Field (Bears Games)

It's been a long time since the Bears played their home games at Wrigley Field, but there was absolutely nothing like it. Basically, you were right on top of the field and you could not only see what was going on but you could almost feel it as well. Things have changed so much in the NFL because there were plenty of other teams that shared baseball stadiums as well. Now it seems that everybody has their own football-only stadium with sky boxes, luxury suites, and all those fancy additions. I'm not going to say those things aren't great if you can afford them, but it was not the real thing that people saw when they were watching a game from Wrigley Field.

Not only were fans close to the action, but the way the stadium was configured, the corner of the end zone included the brick outfield walls. You could catch a touchdown pass in the corner of the end zone and run right into the wall if you weren't careful.

Wrigley Field today is all about baseball. (Well, I guess it's about outdoor hockey on New Year's Day, as well). But back in the day when the Bears were playing there, it felt like football was meant to be. There was no feeling like being among the 40,000 fans at Wrigley for a Bears game. I mean, Chicago fans support their teams, but there's no division when it comes to football. Baseball fans split their loyalties between the White Sox and the Cubs, but everyone roots for the Bears. So back then, the crowd was in full voice, right on top of the game, screaming for the Bears. Of course, we had the 1963 season, but for the most part, the team wasn't very good in the 1960s. Then they moved to Soldier Field, and they weren't much better. But if the Bears were involved in a close game in Wrigley, it was an awesome experience.

> **"Baseball fans split their loyalties between the White Sox and the Cubs, but everyone roots for the Bears."**

The other thing that made Wrigley so great for me is that I got to climb the wall and get into Wrigley and watch the game. It was run by the Park District so I could get in and walk the sidelines, for crying out loud. Can you believe that? I could actually walk on the same sidelines as Mike Ditka, Dick Butkus, Gale Sayers, and Doug Buffone, and feel the game and breathe the game as it was being played. No, they don't make stadiums like that anymore. Try walking the sidelines now and you'll go to jail.

2. Wrigley Field (Baseball)

Whether you are a Cubs fan who loves Wrigley or a Sox fan who can't stand it, you simply cannot overlook Wrigley as one of the great ballparks in big-league baseball and one of the greatest sites in Chicago.

I'm not just talking about what it means from a sports point of view. How many visitors come to Chicago and one of the top places they want to see is Wrigley Field? And it's not just sports fans. People who come to Chicago want to go shopping on Michigan Avenue, they want to see Wrigley Field and they want to go to the Lakefront or eat at a restaurant their friends have told them about (and I think they should go to Wildfire and Gibson's, in that order).

From a baseball perspective, you have to think of all the sellouts and all the years that fans have showed up and all the people that

Any way you look at it, Wrigley Field is one of the great big-league baseball venues. This is Wrigley Field on October 1, 2008, before the start of the ill-fated NLDS between the Cubs and the Los Angeles Dodgers. (AP Photo)

have followed that team for generations. No, they've never won a World Series there. They are still waiting, but it is a great ballpark that means a lot to both the city of Chicago and all of baseball.

3. Chicago Stadium (Basketball and Ice Hockey)

This was one of the true gems of our lifetime. There was never anything like the stadium, and the noise that came from the building when Bobby Hull, Stan Mikita, and Tony Esposito would skate onto the ice was incredible. I think opponents were literally shocked when they came on the ice and heard the reception the Hawks got. In the late 1960s and '70s, there were a lot of loud venues around hockey, but there was nothing close to Chicago Stadium. They may have made noise in New York, Boston, and Philadelphia, but the Hawks' crowds were always two or three times louder than fans in those other cities.

It was the same thing as far as the Bulls were concerned. I'm not just talking about the Michael Jordan era, either. Of course it was loud then—the people responded to Jordan every time he walked on the court and was in full flight. The Jordan who played in the Chicago Stadium was the Jordan who was at the absolute peak of his powers. As he got older and moved across the street to the United Center, he was probably a more mature player who was better at getting his teammates involved, but the Jordan who played at the Stadium was a brilliant athlete with the heart of a lion.

Here's one of the things that stands out to me. I go back all the way to the start of the franchise in the 1966–67 season, but the season that really stands out to me is 1976–77. The Bulls were not a great team back then, but they were good enough to make the playoffs. They met the Portland Trail Blazers in the first round, and that was the Blazer team that had Bill Walton, Maurice Lucas, and a bunch of role players who would go on to win the NBA title. They beat Julius Erving and George McGinnis, and they were an outstanding team.

Well, that championship team had to fight like hell to beat the Bulls. It was a best-of-three series, and the Bulls won the game at the Stadium and pushed it to a third and final game in Portland. I don't think I ever heard a louder crowd at a basketball game than I did that day in 1977. Wilbur Holland was the guy for the Bulls. He was an average player who had a very good season that year. Holland hit two free throws at the end of that game and gave the Bulls a win. That may have been the best environment I have ever been in as a sports fan.

4. Comiskey Park (White Sox)

I'm not saying that going to a White Sox game back in the day was a glamorous experience, but it sure was memorable. Comiskey was a great place to watch a game. A lot of the seats had poles and obstructions, but I didn't care. When you were at Comiskey, you were at a ballpark. You felt like you were at a real baseball stadium. You could smell the hot dogs and the beer and all the other food every time you turned a corner. You could smell a lot of other things, as well.

As a vendor, it was a very difficult location to get to, and you really were taking a chance every time you walked the four blocks from the L stop to the stadium. It's not like it is now where a train takes you right to 35th Street. There was a lot of tension, and there were a lot of racial problems. Those are the facts. It was hard to get to work to vend beer or hot dogs or whatever else you were selling.

But the White Sox were our team, and Comiskey was our ballpark. I remember the doubleheaders, when I was a kid. They played a lot of Sunday doubleheaders and they played a few Friday night twilight-doubleheaders. They don't play many now except when there are rainouts. But there was something special about getting to Comiskey Park early on Sunday knowing that the White Sox were going to play two games. It seemed like you would be there all day.

Venerable Comiskey Park as it looked in 1983. (AP Photo)

What could be better, especially when the Yankees were in town with Mickey Mantle, Roger Maris, and Whitey Ford? The only bad part was when they beat our brains out.

That was baseball in a different era. That was baseball before free agency and the huge contracts that go to benchwarmers and the multi-millions that go to the stars. I'm not saying it was better back then, but it sure was a lot different. Those are the memories that stay with you until the day you die.

5. Thillens Stadium (youth baseball ballpark at the corner of Devon and Kedzie)

I know what most of you are thinking as you read this, "How can this guy list a little league stadium as being one of the best in Chicago?"

I'll tell you how. As far as a little leaguer is concerned, there was nothing like it. To play a game at Thillens was a tremendous thrill for any kid. It was not a little league stadium. It was a real baseball stadium that was built for younger players, and it gave them a special feel for the game. For any Chicago kid playing organized baseball, the idea of playing a game at Thillens Stadium was always your goal. At its peak, Jack Brickhouse would broadcast championship games from Thillens. Can you imagine what a thrill it was not only to play there but to know that Jack was broadcasting the games?

I just loved having the chance to play there. I was a pretty damn good player. I could hit, and I could field—pretty good second baseman. When I was on that field, I wanted to win. That's how I played and if anything, everyone played harder there at Thillens.

It was an amazing place, and Mel Thillens did a great job. It looked like it was about to go under, but the Chicago Park District has kept it going, and it's still a great place to play.

11

All-Time Chicago Baseball Team

I DON'T THINK THIS LIST IS GOING TO SETTLE ANY ARGUMENTS, but it should start a few. I want to include a piece on Chicago's all-time baseball team. For my purposes, I have two all-time teams. The first is the one I would use for one game only. The qualifications for making this group include being a fearsome and feisty player who is not going to get nervous in a big game.

The second is my All-Chicago team, and that one is based on a season's worth of activity. Instead of having to win one game to get into the playoffs, I'm looking at it from the perspective of chemistry and guys who could last the year together and help each other thrive. Many of the players are on both teams, but there are some key differences.

I'm not going to sit here and give you all their stats. You can get those numbers anywhere. I'm going to tell you what I saw in each player.

You Must Win One Game

1B—ERNIE BANKS, CUBS

Ernie may be Mr. Cub and he wants to play two, but when he was up to bat, he was all concentration in the batter's box. People forget how good a hitter Ernie was; they tend to focus on the home runs. That's a big factor, but I remember Ernie being the kind of guy who would adjust really well and get key hits in late-game situations. Not only that, he would get hits on a lot of pitcher's pitches. He didn't have to wait for a mistake to get a base hit.

2B—RYNE SANDBERG, CUBS

He was a nice, personable guy throughout his whole playing career. But now that he's managing in the Cubs' system, you get to see the whole personality a lot more. He will get riled up, and he will stand up for his players. That shows you what his true mentality was when he was a player. He was a battler, and he had confidence in himself. One great game did more for him than just about anything else. The Saturday afternoon game against the Cardinals when he hit two game-tying home runs off Bruce Sutter remains one of the great examples of a player lifting his team to great heights.

SS—LUIS APARICIO, WHITE SOX

Luis was just about the best fielding shortstop ever. A lot of people go with Ozzie Smith from St. Louis and Omar Vizquel, who was great with Cleveland, but you aren't going to get much of an argument when Aparicio's name comes up as far as great fielders go. He would dive for balls and make the tough play, not just the easy ones. He was also a battler at the plate who would bunt, move the runner over, and foul off pitches until he got the one he wanted and then drive it into the gap.

3B—BILL MELTON, WHITE SOX

This might rile a lot of people, but remember the category. We're talking about one game, and while Melton had a few deficiencies— he would struggle in the field—he was tough as a clutch hitter. He had a lot of power at a time when few players could hit the ball for distance. I just want Melton in my lineup because he's going to intimidate the pitcher and make things happen. He might strike out two or three times and he might make an error, but I want Melton up when his team has a chance to tie or win the game.

LF—ALBERT BELLE, WHITE SOX

I know this is one of the most unpopular picks I could make, and that Belle was not very popular in the locker room, either. But when Belle came up to the plate, it didn't matter what the fans thought of him, what his teammates thought of him, or what the media thought of him. He could hit. When he came to the White Sox, he started off poorly. He ended up hitting 49 home runs his second season after totaling just 30 in his first Sox season. I just got the feeling that nobody could pitch to him and nobody wanted to pitch to him. For one game, nobody has to get along with him. They just have to stay on the same field with him for a couple of hours. I think he would do a lot of damage.

CF—KEN BERRY, WHITE SOX

This selection probably says quite a bit about the kind of center fielders we have had in this town throughout the years. Berry is a real stretch on any kind of All-Star team. But we didn't have Willie Mays. We didn't have Mickey Mantle. We didn't have Ken Griffey Jr. in his prime. (I am talking about players who played here when they were at their best, not at the end of their careers.) Berry had a great glove, and that's why I'm going to select him. He played a much shallower center field than they do today because he could go and get it. He would cut off a lot of hits and a lot of extra base hits. His numbers weren't great, but they weren't terrible, either. He made the All-Star team once and won two Gold Gloves.

RF—ANDRE DAWSON, CUBS

Oh, the Hawk was something else when he came to the Cubs. He was probably in his athletic prime during his years with the Montreal Expos, but he could really play with the Cubs. To come to Chicago and win the MVP with a last-place team was amazing—you can argue that a player on a last-place team should never win the MVP and probably win that argument most days. But Dawson was an awesome hitter with the Cubs. He was the kind of guy who could really carry a team when he got on a streak.

C—CARLTON FISK, WHITE SOX

What a player! What a dominant guy! He had a great career with the Red Sox before he came to Chicago for what looked like might be two or three years, maybe five at the outside. However, he played longer with the White Sox than he did with Boston, and that's a tribute to the way he worked out and the kind of condition he kept himself in. To play catcher as long as he did (1969–93) tells you that the man had a lot of pride in what he did, and he was great at what he did. He was a sensitive guy who didn't really get along with the media, but Fisk was everything you want a player to be, and to do it at that grueling position is simply unbelievable.

STARTING PITCHER—FERGUSON JENKINS, CUBS

Simply a dominating pitcher who would do what he had to in order to win. When I say dominating, I don't mean like Bob Gibson or Sandy Koufax. Fergie could strike you out, but he was not that overpowering kind of strikeout pitcher. Instead, he was dominating from the way he walked to the mound. He knew it was his job to win the game. That was the expectation, and he delivered. If it was Willie Mays coming to the plate, if it was Hank Aaron or Roberto Clemente, there was no way that Fergie was going to give in. He would always keep the pitch on the edge of the plate, he threw hard, and he fought to win the battle.

RELIEF PITCHER—BOBBY JENKS, WHITE SOX

There have been some great relief pitchers in this town, such as Bruce Sutter and Lee Smith, but Jenks was the only one who was part of a World Series winner. I like his makeup. He wants the ball, and he is going to throw hard. If you can hit it, fine, but he's not going to change his game plan. Maybe that will change later in his career, but he is still strong, and he throws hard. He believes in challenging the hitter, and he has won that battle a lot in his young career.

DH—FRANK THOMAS, WHITE SOX

It's pretty clear that Frank in his prime was the best hitter the White Sox ever had. It's also just as clear that he was no kind of fielder at first base. He could actually catch the ball fairly well, but he had about the worst throwing arm I can ever remember at first base. If he had to throw the ball, it was an adventure. But as far as hitting went, he could crush it and he was always patient waiting for his pitch. He may have been a little too patient at times, but that's probably why he was such a great hitter. But for one game, I can't afford to play him in the field.

For an Entire Season

Let's look at the all-time Chicago team from the perspective of a season. It's quite a bit different than the first team.

1B—FRANK THOMAS, WHITE SOX

I figure that over the course of a season, Frank's glove—really his arm—is not going to be as big an issue. I want him in the lineup, and I could have had him at DH, but if I stick him at first, I can put Ernie at shortstop and make a couple of other key moves, as well.

2B—NELLIE FOX, WHITE SOX

I've never seen a better fielding second baseman, and that's why I need Fox in the lineup for the full season. He was a complete player, too. He could get his bat on the ball, and he could hit in the clutch. But he was a beautiful fielder. He could get to everything, and he was always accurate when he got rid of the ball. Nobody turned a double play like Nellie.

Nellie Fox was one of the best fielding second basemen ever to wear a uniform in Chicago. This photo was taken in 1953. (AP photo)

SS—ERNIE BANKS, CUBS

This was the position where he won his MVPs and when Ernie was in his prime, he was a great hitting, great fielding shortstop. He was among the best in the game, maybe not quite as good a hitter as Alex Rodriguez, but he was great and a very good fielder. I could see him turning the double play with Fox, and they would have been smooth together.

3B—RON SANTO, CUBS

Overall, Santo was a better player than Bill Melton. He could do it all, and he was an excellent fielder, as well. Santo was one of the best clutch hitters of his time. Maybe he should be in the Hall of Fame, but that's not what we're talking about here. He was the best all-around third baseman in Chicago history.

LF—BILLY WILLIAMS, CUBS
Billy had the sweetest swing of his time, and he was a great all-around player. He could hit for average or with power, and he was a really good fielder who could make the catch and then make the throw on the money. Talk about being a clutch hitter—I would rather have Billy Williams up in a clutch situation than just about anyone else.

CF—CHET LEMON, WHITE SOX
Just like in the situation where we wanted to win one game, this is not the strongest category for Chicago. Lemon had a little bit more speed, a little bit more power, and was a better hitter. At his best, he wasn't quite the fielder that Berry was, but he was very good.

RF—ANDRE DAWSON, CUBS

STARTING PITCHER—FERGIE JENKINS, CUBS

RELIEF PITCHER—BOBBY JENKS, WHITE SOX

DH—RYNE SANDBERG, CUBS
It might seem strange to have Ryno at designated hitter because he was a great second baseman and he did a solid job in the field. However, I don't think he was as good as Nellie Fox. To me, that guy was a magician who could make every play imaginable. You don't remember Ryno getting dirty too often. Some people might say that's because he was such a great athlete that he could get to the ball without getting dirty, but I want to know that my second baseman will make the play and do whatever he has to in order to make the out. Nothing against Sandberg, but I'll take Fox as my second baseman and Ryno as the DH.

12

All-Time Bears Team

ALL-TIME TEAMS SERVE A REAL PURPOSE besides taking a trip down memory lane and playing the "remember when" game. Tony Soprano never liked playing that game, and he called it the lowest form of conversation. But by putting together an all-time Chicago Bears team, you get a chance to set the standards of who has been the best player at each position. In some cases, the answers might seem obvious, but in other cases, it's not as clear cut.

I'll defend my choices, and I'll take these guys on the field wearing Bears uniforms any day of the week.

All-Time Bears Offensive Team

QB—SID LUCKMAN

When your all-time quarterback had his prime in the 1940s, that has to say a few things. One is pretty obvious: the Bears have had medio-cre and below-average quarterback play for a very long time. The number of guys who have excelled for the Bears at the quarterback position over a number of years since Luckman's career ended in 1950 is exactly zero. I'm not saying they haven't had a couple of good quarterbacks along the way, but they haven't had any great ones. Jim McMahon was a Super Bowl–winning quarterback and might have been a great one, but he was always hurt. Erik Kramer put good

189

numbers together, but he was not great. He was a pretty good quarterback who had one very good year with the Bears.

It's not fair to Luckman to go on about how bad the Bears quarterbacks were after he retired. He was clearly the man for the Bears, and George Halas absolutely loved him. He was smart, tough, and accurate, and he came to play every game and every year. I didn't see him play because he finished before I was born, but I certainly know about his accomplishments. The Bears won four NFL titles when he was quarterback, and who do you think was under center when the Bears beat the Redskins 73–0 in the 1940 NFL Championship Game? It was Luckman, my friend. He's still the all-time leader in yards and touchdowns. And that goofy passer rating system they use? No Bears quarterback has had a better passer rating than Luckman did when he finished the 1943 season with a 107.8 mark. Think about how good and accurate he was.

It would be nice if the team had at least a few other quarterbacks to compare with Luckman, but that doesn't diminish what he did back then. He really was outstanding.

RUNNING BACKS—WALTER PAYTON AND GALE SAYERS

If the Bears have not had their share of great quarterbacks, they have dominated the running back position. The Bears are so strong here that I am making Red Grange my return specialist, and he barely beats out Devin Hester there. Think about it. A lot of people credit Grange as being the main force in the National Football League becoming a viable professional sports league. When he played, pro football was almost an afterthought—college football, baseball, and boxing were the sports that most people followed.

Payton makes the list because he had so much heart and the skills to do everything on the football field. He was more than just a natural—he had great athletic ability, but you don't become a great football player simply on your natural talent. You have to work to

One of the greatest running backs ever, Walter Payton (34) takes off with the ball during first-half action on December 20, 1987, in Chicago against the Seattle Seahawks. (AP Photo/John Swart)

develop it, and that's what Walter Payton did. He was a runner, he was a receiver, he could pass, and he could block. He was great in all of these categories, and he was a dominant professional who wanted the Bears to win. He was a great practical joker—I think a lot of people know that—but when the Bears were in a position to win the championship in 1985, Payton made sure they didn't get distracted and didn't perform at anything less than their absolute best on the football field. Maybe it was for selfish purposes because he had put in so many years on bad teams, but Walter always wanted to win a championship and he led his team to one in 1985.

I love Gale Sayers. He was such a great back who had so much pride in what he did. And what he did, nobody else could do. Barry Sanders may have come close with the Lions, but he didn't have the pure magic that Gale did when he ran with the football. I will say that he can be a little sensitive at times, and he definitely doesn't like to take a backseat to any back—including Walter—but he's also a great guy with a sense of humor. Some people don't understand him, but that's their problem and not his. He was just a superior talent who ran hard every game he played, and it's too bad that knee injuries prevented us from seeing even more from him. He was the goods. He was one of the best players ever.

WIDE RECEIVERS—JOHNNY MORRIS AND WILLIE GAULT

Everybody talks about how poor the Bears have been at the quarterback position, but it isn't like we've had a bunch of Jerry Rices playing wideout for the Bears, either. Morris was a legitimate receiver. A really talented pro who was good at his job, Morris was a difference-maker. But did he have the same kind of talent or ability as Rice or Randy Moss? I don't think so, and I don't think Johnny Morris would argue that fact. But he was a very good receiver who caught just about anything he got his hands on.

Willie Gault was fast and could stretch the defense better than any receiver the Bears have had before or since. That's not surprising because he was a track guy, a hurdler. He could run like the wind, and if you caught him on the right day, he could really make a huge difference. I don't think there were a lot of those games—certainly not enough of them. Let's face it: when it came to contact, Willie didn't like it. He wasn't about sticking his nose in there to make a block or anything like that. But he could do it as a receiver and a kickoff returner. The Minnesota game in the 1985 season is probably his best game. That's the game where McMahon came off the bench and Gault caught the TD pass that gave the Bears the spark that almost let them go undefeated. He ran back a kickoff against the Redskins when he was about twice as fast as any player the Bears had. But to put him on the all-time Bears teams tells you how much the team has lacked at the wide receiver position.

TIGHT END—MIKE DITKA

Who else could you have at tight end for the Bears? Before he was Da Coach, he was one of the two guys in the NFL who really defined the position. You had John Mackey of the Colts, who was truly great, and a guy Mike always praises, and you had Ditka. Ditka was just as good as Mackey if not better, but I don't think you would ever hear Ditka say that. I think he is happy to give the nod to Mackey.

But Ditka was great. He was this bull of a blocker and one hell of a receiver. He wanted the ball, and he was not about to go down from an arm tackle. You had to really stick him to bring him down, and most times it was two or three guys that brought him down. He was hungry, nasty, and tough, and he knew how to play. You could see that he would get upset if the other guys on the team weren't playing with the same effort, and that's probably what made him such an effective coach for the Bears. You can't tolerate mediocrity. Ditka didn't when he was a player, and he certainly didn't as a coach.

OFFENSIVE TACKLES—JIM COVERT AND KEITH VAN HORNE

Okay, I'll admit it. When it comes to the '85 Bears, I'm a little bit biased. I love those guys. It was just an awesome team overall, and I think you would be hard-pressed to find a better aspect to the team that the offensive line. Those guys were great talents who really worked well together. To me, Covert was one of the best tackles who ever played. I'm not going to get into the Hall of Fame argument because if you look at the voting, it's just a couple of football writers who sit in a room the day before the Super Bowl and make their cases and decide who's good enough to get in and who isn't. Basically, if you have somebody who is good at arguing and can make your case, you can get in. But anybody who watched this team play knows that Covert could do the job as a pass blocker and a run blocker. He protected Jim McMahon's backside, and he did a great job. Van Horne was a dominant guy, as well, a really good run blocker. When he made a couple of good blocks early in the game, the running game would kick in and never stop.

OFFENSIVE GUARDS—TOM THAYER AND MARK BORTZ

If the Bears offensive linemen were underrated in general, then these two guys in particular didn't get their share of the credit. When you could run the way the Bears could with Walter Payton and Matt Suhey, it's because you could block, and these two guys excelled. They could pull and lead the sweeps, and when Thayer and Bortz went for a linebacker or a defensive back, they didn't miss. They were plenty tough and nasty, but I thought they were also really skilled guys who gave their all every Sunday so the Bears would get the win. These guys never had any reason to feel ashamed because they played so hard.

CENTER—OLIN KREUTZ

Don't get me wrong—I don't think you could go wrong with Jay Hilgenberg. I said I was prejudiced towards the '85 Bears, but looking at it as fairly and objectively as I can, I have to give the nod to Kreutz. As nasty as he can be on the field, he's the kind of guy who makes his teammates listen and do the right thing. Not that he's perfect and hasn't had a few problems with botched snaps over the years. But you know what? You can live with that because he's such a madman as a blocker. He's pretty devastating, playing hard and going for the throat. Not really much different than Hilgenberg, but the big difference is that Jay was surrounded by great blockers who stayed together season after season. That's not the case anymore. You can never have enough good offensive linemen, and the cast keeps changing. That's part of what makes Kreutz so good. He has different guys around him from season to season, and his play stays at a high level.

All-Time Bears Defensive Team

DEFENSIVE ENDS—RICHARD DENT AND DAN HAMPTON

Dent is one of the best rushers in NFL history. He got after the quarterback with his speed and quickness, and the guy was literally hungry. He had those bad teeth when he came to the Bears, and they sent him to the dentist. When they fixed his teeth, he could eat whatever he wanted and he put on weight, got stronger, and was virtually unstoppable when he turned the corner. Maybe he wasn't as good as Bruce Smith (in Buffalo), but he was pretty close.

Hampton was the man. You could put him at defensive tackle and maybe that was his best position, but you don't lose a thing by putting him in at end and that way, you can get Steve McMichael in the lineup, as well. Hampton was a dominant and great football player who was as good against the run as any defensive end who ever played the game. Not that he didn't rush the passer well, but he just took it personally if you tried to run to his side of the field—that wasn't going to happen.

This is another spot where the Bears are absolutely stocked. I have Dent and Hampton, but that means I can't put Doug Atkins in the lineup, and the stories about that guy are legendary. He was as strong as anybody who has ever worn a Bears uniform, and he could take over a game with his size and strength. Atkins was another great football player, but I'm going with my guys Hampton and Dent.

DEFENSIVE TACKLES—WALLY CHAMBERS
AND STEVE McMICHAEL

You want to know how good Wally Chambers was? Take a look at Lee Roy Selmon, who made the Hall of Fame playing defensive tackle for the Bucs in the 1970s and '80s. Chambers was just as good as Selmon and probably should be in the Hall of Fame. He was strong and fast for such a big guy, and he could get in the backfield to collapse the pocket in an instant.

Everybody likes to think of McMichael as this wild man who scared the crap out of people because of the things he did when he was on television. He was just taking advantage of the situation, and he was a showman. He wanted to make a couple extra bucks and you can't blame anyone for that. But there were no gimmicks when he was on the field. He was all business all the way. He was a hard working guy, too. He played with Hampton, and I think Hampton might have been a little bit more talented, but McMichael made it up with his intelligence on the field, and his hard work made things happen.

MIDDLE LINEBACKER—DICK BUTKUS

The best of the best. I think Dick Butkus was the most dominant defensive player to ever wear a uniform in the National Football League, and I don't think anyone else even comes close. A lot of people will talk about Lawrence Taylor, and I know he was a damn good player, but he had his problems and off-the-field distractions. He could have been even better than he was. Butkus, on the other hand, got everything out of his body that it had to give. When he was healthy and playing his best football, Butkus was on a different level. Dave Wannstedt always used to use an expression, saying he wanted guys who were "flying around" and making plays. Well, that was Butkus.

He was absolutely ferocious and could not be distracted. All he wanted to do was show he was the best guy on the football field every time he stepped on it. You weren't going to run on Dick Butkus. He just wouldn't allow it. Challenge Butkus and he would destroy you. He was stronger, tougher, and meaner than just about everybody he went up against. On the field, he loved beating the hell out of people. Other guys who played with him were in awe of him, and guys who played against him were afraid of him.

You don't see too much of that in the NFL. Maybe some people were afraid of Taylor and Mean Joe Greene in Pittsburgh, but I think just about everybody was afraid of Butkus. He was a brutal hitter, and he would come with everything he had all the time.

The Bears have had plenty of other great middle linebackers. If they were on other teams, Bill George and Mike Singletary might be the best on those teams. George almost invented the way the middle linebacker plays football, and Singletary was the perfect guy to play the middle on the '85 Bears. Singletary had the benefit of playing behind Hampton and McMichael, but don't take anything away from him. He was able to take advantage of that situation. Both George and Singletary are in the Hall of Fame. That tells you everything you need to know about the Bears and the middle linebacker situation.

Brian Urlacher? Good player but nowhere near Butkus, George, and Singletary. I don't see Urlacher being as physical as the other guys. He's way too sensitive and thin-skinned. He should not let criticism bother him so much, and he sure as hell shouldn't say that the people who are criticizing him don't know football. Oh really? Is that the case? Well, Bears fans know about great middle linebacking play, and they ain't getting it from you. That's one thing we do know. Urlacher has had his moments and he has been good, and at times very good, but he is just not in the category of those Hall of Famers.

OUTSIDE LINEBACKERS—WILBER MARSHALL AND DOUG BUFFONE

I really think Marshall might have been the key player in the '85 Bears defense. He was so athletic and ferocious that there was just no getting away from him. I don't have any proof of it for sure, but I think that when teams played the Bears back then, the guy quarterbacks were looking for was Marshall. He was an angry man on the field, and he made guys pay on an every-week basis. He could rush the quarterback, he could drop into coverage, and he could tackle. What more do you want? He had the signature moment of that NFC Championship Game win over the Rams when he picked up the fumble from Dieter Brock and ran it in for a touchdown with the snow coming down. (What the hell kind of name is "Dieter" anyway?) Marshall got the glory that time, and he deserved it.

Doug was just an awesome player. You know he's been on the radio so long and he's done a great job and a lot of fans never had a chance to see him play. But it's got to tell you something that he played next to Butkus and knew how to work with him so that Butkus was at his best. You'd never get Doug to take any credit for anything Butkus ever did on the field, but the bottom line is that they worked great together. Doug was a great player on his own, and he was a great tackler. Listen to him on the radio and he'll talk about the fundamentals and how important it is to be able to tackle. Well, Doug's one guy who played as good a game as he talked. He had the fundamentals down. He was also good in coverage, and he had the hands to make interceptions.

CORNERBACKS—BENNIE McRAE AND ALLAN ELLIS

I think the '85 Bears were superior to the '63 Bears, but not at all positions, and cornerback was one of them. Leslie Frazier was good, no doubt about that, and Mike Richardson was good enough, considering the pass rush that they had. But McRae was something else in the 1960s. They didn't use the term cover corner back then because a corner was expected to do more than cover the wide receiver. McRae was a heck of a tackler, and he stuck with receivers like glue. He got the job done.

Ellis played for Bears teams that weren't great. They struggled to compete, and they were basically pretty ordinary back in the 1970s (Ellis wore a Bears uniform from 1973–77 and 1979–80), but he was one of the most underrated players you ever saw. He was good, and he played hard. Maybe he wasn't an All-Pro, but I really liked him. You could depend on him.

SAFETIES—GARY FENCIK AND MIKE BROWN

Both guys were plenty smart and instinctive on the field. That's what you need from your safeties: guys who can anticipate what the next play will be so they can be in the right position most of the time. Fencik understood offenses, and that's why he was in the right position. Same thing with Brown. Injuries have cost him quite a bit over the years, but he's been a clutch player and smart guy for a long time. Brown's highlights were returning those two interceptions for back-to-back winners in overtime back in 2001. Some guys have a knack for being in the right spot at the right time, and Brown is one of them.

All-Time Special Teams

PUNTER—BOBBY JOE GREEN

He is basically a forgotten man because he punted such a long time ago, but he could kick it a long way, and he was dependable.

PLACEKICKER—ROBBIE GOULD

It's close and you wouldn't go too far wrong if you took Kevin Butler, but Gould just seems more consistent. It would be good if he could kick one for 50 yards or more every so often, but I'll take what he gives us. Who expected anything from Gould when he came out of Penn State? But he is the real deal.

RETURN SPECIALIST—RED GRANGE

This would seem the obvious spot for Devin Hester because he may very well be the best kickoff and punt returner in NFL history, but I will take Grange. He's the guy that George Halas turned to when pro football got established as a big-time sport, and you have to give him credit. He sold tickets because people wanted to see him make plays, and that's what he did. He was the greatest open-field runner in the history of football, and that's why I go with him as my return specialist.

13

Top 5 Chicago Athletes and One More

The Best Chicago Athlete—Michael Jordan

Chicago has had some incredible athletes. Some guys had skills that made it nearly impossible to stop them, some guys lifted their teammates on their shoulders, and some athletes had incredible charisma. They were the kind of guys who gave you goosebumps when they stepped on the court, the ice, or the field. You know something incredible was going to happen, and they rarely disappointed.

The best athlete to wear a Chicago uniform is obvious. I have to go with Michael Jordan. I'd give him a slight edge over Bobby Hull. It might shock some people that I have Hull not only so high on the list but so close to Jordan, but that's the way I see it.

Let's get back to Jordan. I've said for many years that I've always thought that Wilt Chamberlain was the best basketball player I've ever seen. I never meant that as an insult to Michael. I'm not complaining about Jordan, and it's not a negative comment about Jordan. It's just that Chamberlain averaged better than 50 points a game for the season and he played 48 minutes every night.

Michael had this amazing athletic ability that was obvious the first time you saw him play at North Carolina. He hit the game-winning shot in the National Championship Game as a freshman. Everything good that ever happened to Jordan he used and built off it and became better. He hit that shot. He hit the shot over Ehlo to get it started against Cleveland. He hit so many game winners against Cleveland that it's hard to keep track of them all. He kept hitting game winners throughout his career all the way through that final championship against the Jazz when he gave Bryon Russell that little push, cleared himself, and rose up for the winner. Just beautiful.

What it comes down to for Jordan is how competitive he was on the court and in just about anything he ever did. He loved to win, but he hated to lose even more. As great an athlete as he was in his prime, it was that desire and that hatred of losing that kept him so productive. I don't know that there's ever been any pro athlete in any sport who could match that fire to play at such a high level. I guess Larry Bird and Magic Johnson had the same kind of hatred of losing, but they were not like Jordan when it came to producing, and both of them had better supporting casts.

> "I don't know that there's ever been any pro athlete in any sport who could match that fire to play at such a high level."

Jordan the athlete was just an amazing guy to watch. Remember, the Jordan who was winning championships was older. When the Bulls won their first title in 1991, Jordan was already 28 years old. I'm not saying that's old, but he had already been in the league since 1984. He had been around, and he had seen and been a part of a lot of things. I think that championship had as much to do with what was going on inside his mind as his athletic talent.

Jordan's athletic ability was always on display, but the first three or four years of his career were something else. It was his second year that he broke his foot, and he had to miss most of the season. The Bulls managed to make the playoffs, and Jordan was able to come back and play against Boston. He was as fresh as he could be in that series, and he scored 63 points in that second game. That's a record that nobody has come close to, and I don't know if anyone will. Jordan basically kept the Bulls in the game all by himself, and that's when the Celtics had Bird, Kevin McHale, and Robert Parish. It was one of the greatest athletic displays that I've ever seen.

The Second-Best Chicago Athlete—Bobby Hull

Hull is next, and I'm not going to apologize for that, not for a second. Hull was this dominant hockey player who had as much charisma as any Chicago athlete I ever saw. I know his son Brett scored more NHL goals, and there are other hockey players who supposedly rank higher than Bobby Hull. Most people say Wayne Gretzky, while some say Bobby Orr. Those people are all wrong. Hull was the best and most dominant of all of them when he was at the top of his game.

When Hull climbed those stairs and stepped on the ice, the roar from the crowd would not stop. The Blackhawks fans loved him and loved watching him play. It was the speed he had when he stepped on the ice, the power of his slap shots, and the viciousness of his game. Combine all those things and you have the greatest hockey player ever when he was in his prime.

Gretzky understood the game probably better than anyone, he could pass like nobody else, and he could put it in the net. But even his biggest supporters are not going to talk about Gretzky as some kind of physical presence because he was not. He wasn't going to hit anyone, and he wasn't going to stand up for himself. Whether he was with Edmonton or Los Angeles, the team always had some kind of enforcer to stand next to him or stand up for him. And you can't tell me that being physical is not a big part of hockey. Tell that to somebody else because I'm not buying it. Gretzky was great at what he did, but he did not do everything and that's the bottom line. A lot of people may not like it, but that's the truth.

I'm not going to say anything bad about Orr because he was a dynamic skater, he changed the game, and he was physical. But the bottom line is that he got hurt and he was not able to do it for as long as Hull, so I'm going to give Hull the edge.

There was nothing like watching Hull take the puck in his own end and get that wind up as he started moving down the ice. It was sheer power. Nobody wanted to get in his way, and when they did, they were not about to stop him. As he would approach the blue line, you knew he was thinking about letting that slap shot go. He'd stride over the line and the next thing you knew, that stick was past his ear and then rocketing forward. I don't think opposing goalies often saw it because he shot so hard. They were either in the way of the shot or it would rip into the net or off the post.

That's another thing about Hull. When a shot goes off the post, it's a pretty loud and distinct sound. But when one of Hull's shots went off the post, it was like a gunshot. *Nobody* ever shot the puck as hard as Bobby Hull.

The Third-Best Chicago Athlete—Ernie Banks

The third-best athlete on my list is Ernie Banks. On the surface, it doesn't seem that Ernie was the same kind of athlete as Jordan or Hull or the two guys coming next, but Banks was an All-Star at shortstop and first base.

Banks was the kind of player they didn't have back in the 1950s. He was a shortstop who could hit and hit with power. Today, you have guys like Alex Rodriguez, who has since moved to third, but he was a shortstop with power. When Nomar Garciaparra came up with the Red Sox and Derek Jeter came up with the Yankees, they were shortstops who could really hit and had a little pop, as well. I guess Cal Ripken is the guy who really changed things around as far as the shortstops are concerned. He was big and strong, and he had power.

Ernie Banks, shown here in a photo from April 1969, was one of the first shortstops who could hit with power. (AP Photo)

There was a time when you had guys like Bud Harrelson, Mark Belanger, and Eddie Brinkman playing shortstop. Their job was to catch the baseball and make a throw. If they got a hit once in a while, that was great, but their job was to field the ball and make a play.

That's why Ernie was so amazing. He played at a time when the shortstop was not going to hit for power. That was neither his job nor his concern. Well, somebody forgot to tell Ernie because he was a guy who had pop throughout his career, and that included when he was playing shortstop.

The guy won a couple of MVP awards, for crying out loud. How can anyone say that Banks wasn't one of the greatest shortstops ever, and is there any doubt that he was miles ahead of his time? And it's not like he sacrificed defense, either. The guy could really field, and he won a Gold Glove. He went to the All-Star Game almost every year. He was as complete a player as you could ever find.

Everybody talks about what a nice guy he was, and everyone remembers him for saying "Let's play two," because he enjoyed playing so much. But he wasn't out for a walk in the park. He was a real player. He hit 47 homers in a season, and that's as many as Hank Aaron ever hit in a year. So don't let anyone tell you he wasn't one of Chicago's best athletes.

The Fourth- and Fifth-Best Chicago Athletes— Gayle Sayers and Walter Payton

As far as Chicago's best athletes are concerned, you also have to include Gale Sayers and Walter Payton. It's hard to split them, but I'll go with Sayers as No. 4 and Payton as No. 5. Both guys were just great players and great people. I still love Sayers, and I appreciated everything about Payton.

We had Payton on the show with Dan Jiggetts and myself many times, and I knew him well. He was just a great guy and always full of life and enthusiasm. That was the thing about Walter. He could give you a hard time and bust your chops, but he wouldn't do anything if he wasn't having a good time. So when he would come on our show every week, Dan and I knew he was enjoying himself. But enough reminiscing about the personalities and the radio show—let's get back to these two unbelievable backs and what they did on the field.

Has any team ever had two backs as good as Sayers and Payton? Go back to 1965 when Sayers came into the league. Name each team's best pair of running backs and tell me that any team had as good a pair as Payton and Sayers. You can't find a better pair, and it's just that simple.

Sayers was just a remarkable guy who was faster, quicker, and more instinctive than just about any back that ever played. A lot of people might try to make an argument for Barry Sanders, and he was great, but he was not Sayers. Sayers was faster, and he was bigger. As far as moves and quickness are concerned, Sayers would not have to take a back seat to Sanders. Maybe they were even in that category if you want to give Sanders the benefit of the doubt. But Sayers was the better and scarier back.

He was a guy who was head and shoulders more talented than the other great pros he went up against. It's rare to find that kind of athletic ability anywhere in sports, let alone in football where you usually end up winning a game because you outsmarted the other guy, outexecuted him, or capitalized on his mistake. But to flat-out beat them because you run faster and you have better instincts? That's unbelievable. That's just who Gale Sayers was throughout the early part of his career before he ruined his knee. He didn't have the benefit of the medical advances they have today or else his prime would have lasted a lot longer. But anyone who saw him play even a few games when he was at his peak saw one of the most spectacular athletes ever.

Walter Payton did not have Gale's incredible physical gifts. He was a great athlete and a hard worker and incredibly tough, but he really had to work at it compared to Sayers. And I know Gale is sensitive about that because he worked hard, too. But that's just the way it is. Sayers worked hard to get everything out of his athletic ability, but I would say Payton got everything he had and maybe a little bit more.

 "Walter Payton did not have Gale's incredible physical gifts."

Who could possibly do everything like Walter? I don't just mean his running style where he would hit a linebacker with a stiff arm like Joe Frazier, but the fact that he blocked like an offensive lineman and he could also go out and catch it. He could handle the screen passes, the circle routes, and he could go downfield, too. He did whatever he had to in order to win. Remember Payton throwing the option pass? He had a great arm, and he was accurate. Mike Ditka has always said that Payton was the most complete player he ever saw, and I'm not going to argue with him. He's right. Walter did it all, and his teammates wanted to play with him and get him a championship.

Don't get me wrong. The idea of winning a championship in 1985 was for the team and for themselves, but there was not a player on that team who didn't want to get Payton a title before he retired. That's one of the reasons that year was so great. The Bears won the title for one of the greatest athletes this town has ever seen.

And One More

As far as pure athletes go, those guys are my Top 5. But as far as I'm concerned, I have to throw in one more. Complain about my math if you want to, but I'm adding a sixth, and his name is Dick Butkus.

Butkus is a guy who carried the Bears for many years and he played defense the way they don't do it today. There are great players now and great athletes, but *there has never been a more ferocious player in any sport* than Butkus was when he was in his prime.

I don't care what anyone says. They may all deny it now, but when teams came in here to play the Bears at Wrigley Field in the late 1960s, guys were scared at the thought of playing against Butkus. He was that mean and ferocious. And it was no act—he was like that on game days, and it was all natural. Ask Doug Buffone. He lined up next to Butkus for years, and he saw the ferocity and the way he came to play every single game.

It wasn't just the attitude, either. He was a skilled player who tackled hard and he did it with everything he had. What made him truly special was how fast he would get to the ball carrier. It was just this ability he had to throw away the blockers, find the ball carrier, and absolutely bury him. You do that once or twice early in the game and that running back doesn't feel like running hard any more. It's not

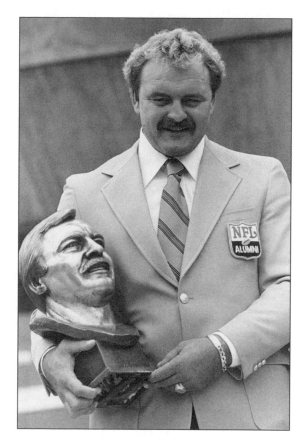

Dick Butkus holds his trophy during enshrinement ceremonies at the Pro Football Hall of Fame in Canton, Ohio, on Saturday, July 28, 1979. (AP Photo)

necessarily his fault, either. That's what Butkus would do. He would take the heart out of a running back or a receiver who caught a short pass and smash it to bits.

They don't do that anymore. How often do you see a linebacker help a running back up after making the tackle? It happens every game and often. That's the kind of thing Butkus never would have done because he was trying to take someone's head off, not help them get up.

Now that was an athlete.

Afterword: The Best Season Ever

THE 1985 BEARS ARE ONE OF THE MOST LEGENDARY TEAMS IN SPORTS.
Much has been written and said about them—including in this
book—and I think we've gone a little overboard when it comes to
their success. Everybody knows they should have been able to win at
least one more title and may even more than that, but they didn't. So
the question becomes—are the '85 Bears the greatest one-year team
in sports?

I'm here to tell you that it's not even close. Not only are those
Bears not the greatest one-year team in sports history, they are not
even the greatest one-year team in Chicago's history. And I'm not
going back to the 1906 Cubs who won 116 games and lost the World
Series to the White Sox or anything like that.

The best one-year team was Michael Jordan's 1995–96 team, the
one that began the second three-peat and the team that went 72–10.
Nobody can win them all, but I swear that season Jordan wanted to.
Almost all of those 10 losses were close games, and the Bulls were
fighting every night. That kind of record is simply amazing in basketball. If a team plays poorly for a five-minute stretch, they can be
hopelessly out of a game. That never happened with these Bulls.

They were extremely motivated from the start. That was Jordan's
first full season back after his little trip to the baseball diamond. He

had come back at the end of the 1994–95 season and been in the playoffs with the Bulls, but they lost, and it was obviously something they were not used to when Jordan was in the lineup. He was determined that there was going to be no sad song at the end of the 1995–96 season.

Jerry Krause and Jerry Reinsdorf did their part. The Bulls' teams prior to that season had some grit and some fire, but not enough of it. They recognized this fact and decided to take a chance and bring in Dennis Rodman. Rodman was one of the league's bad boys at the time and they traded a nice guy like Will Perdue for him. It turned out to be just the move the Bulls needed because Rodman gave them a certain presence and identity they didn't have and he could really rebound—and do it in clutch situations.

You have to give credit to Toni Kukoc that season because he had to adjust to Jordan and Rodman. If anything, Scottie Pippen played his best basketball that season, as well. I'm not just talking about his stats. He had been the team's main man during Jordan's absence, but he went back to being the No. 2 guy and it may have been the one time that he didn't complain.

How good were the Bulls that season? Well, they had one blowout loss to the Knicks in New York late in the regular season. That was the only game they were out of all season. Besides that game, they never lost a game by more than 10 points. They set a record with the 72 wins, they won 33 games on the road, they lost only two games at home, and they won by big margins—an average of 12.2 points per night.

So you have to love that team and you have to give them the edge over the 1985 Bears. The 2007 Patriots went undefeated before they lost in the Super Bowl and there have been other teams that went 15–1 and won the Super Bowl. So as good and tough as the '85 Bears were, they did not set the record. The 72–10 Bulls did, and I'm not saying that mark will never be broken, but it will be a long, long time. Teams like the Boston Celtics and Los Angeles Lakers get off to a good start and the talk is that they will break that record. But all it takes is a bad week or two and those chances disappear. Those Bulls had one bad game all season—and that was it.

It was the best year ever by any Chicago team.